S0-EXA-405

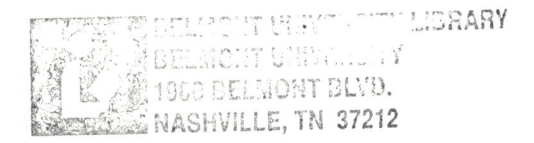

BELMONT UNIVERSITY LIBRARY
BELMONT UNIVERSITY
1900 BELMONT BLVD.
NASHVILLE, TN 37212

The Presidents and the Bible

The Presidents and the Bible

Meditations on the Bible Texts Used by
Our Presidents, from Lincoln to Carter,
at Their Inaugurations

J. W. STORER
New Material by William J. Fallis

Portrait Sketches by T. Victor Hall
and Dean Shelton

BROADMAN PRESS
Nashville, Tennessee

These Historic Scriptures

© Copyright 1952 • Broadman Press

Revised Edition
© Copyright 1976 • Broadman Press
All rights reserved

Updated Edition
© Copyright 1977 • Broadman Press
All rights reserved

Unless otherwise indicated, all Scripture quotations in this book are taken from the American Standard Version of the Bible.

4269-17
ISBN: 0-8054-6917-6

Dewey Decimal Classification: 242
Subject Headings: PRESIDENTS—U.S./RELIGION
Printed in the United States of America

192992
BELMONT UNIVERSITY LIBRARY

PREFACE

It is not generally known that each President of the United States carefully selects the passage of Scripture which is used at his inauguration. Research done in preparation for this book has revealed another interesting fact: until President Grant's first term, no official record was kept of the passages that were used. I have, however, been able to find those which were used by a number of the Presidents before Grant.

We live in a national era which had its distinct beginning with the presidency of Abraham Lincoln. Indeed, there is a very real truth in the statement that our nation was born, not on July 4, 1776, but on April 9, 1865. Whether the nation was a confederation of states up to the time of the surrender at Appomattox is debatable; there is no doubt that after that it was the United States of America. Because of that fact, I have elected, in this study of the Scripture passages used by the Presidents in their inaugurations, to begin with that chosen by Abraham Lincoln.

Preceding a discussion of each Scripture selection, there is given a brief sketch of the President who used it. In those instances where there were two terms, it was necessary to make an arbitrary choice as to which passage would be discussed—a difficulty which did not occur, by the way, with Franklin D. Roosevelt, who chose the same passage for each of his four inaugurations.

That there will be those who dismiss the kissing of the Bible as a concession to religion on the part of our Presidents, I am aware. I myself, however, have no doubt that each of our Presidents selected a Scripture passage with real feeling and that it was with deep humility that he bowed his head and pressed to his lips the Word of God.

Whatever history may record as to the achievements or failures of any President and his administration is another thing entirely. After all, the elevation of a man to the highest office in the gift of the people does not divest him of the fallibilities which are a part of every man's nature.

But I believe that each of our Presidents, past and present, would gladly subscribe to the words of Abraham Lincoln:

"Let us have faith that right makes might, and in that faith let us to the end, dare to do our duty as we understand it."

J. W. STORER

Tulsa, Oklahoma

ACKNOWLEDGMENTS

To Senators Elmer Thomas and Robert S. Kerr, of Oklahoma, who so kindly aided in research; to Robert C. Gooch, chief, General Reference and Bibliography of the Legislative Reference Service, United States Government; to my secretary, Miss Vera Mae Chapman, for painstaking and accurate preparation of the manuscript; and to my wife for her careful, considerate proof reading, I am greatly indebted, and sincerely appreciative.

NOTE FOR NEW EDITION

The first edition of this book, published in 1952 was entitled *These Historic Scriptures*. The six sections on Presidents from Eisenhower to Carter were prepared by William J. Fallis at our request to bring the book up to date.

THE PUBLISHER

CONTENTS

Abraham Lincoln 1
Andrew Johnson 9
Ulysses S. Grant 17
Rutherford B. Hayes 25
James A. Garfield 33
Chester A. Arthur 41
Grover Cleveland 49
Benjamin Harrison 57
William McKinley 65
Theodore Roosevelt 73
William H. Taft 81
Woodrow Wilson 89
Warren G. Harding 97
Calvin Coolidge 105
Herbert Hoover 113
Franklin D. Roosevelt 121
Harry S Truman 129
Dwight Eisenhower 137
John F. Kennedy 145
Lyndon Johnson 153
Richard M. Nixon 161
Gerald Ford 169
Jimmy Carter 175

Abraham Lincoln

President

March 4, 1861—April 15, 1865

REVELATION 16:7

And I heard the altar saying, Yea, O Lord God, the Almighty, true and righteous are thy judgments.

Abraham Lincoln

Abraham Lincoln

Born February 12, 1809, Hardin County (now Larue County), Kentucky.

Died April 15, 1865, Washington, D. C.

A self-schooled lawyer, Abraham Lincoln became a member of the Illinois legislature and of the United States Congress. His series of debates with Stephen A. Douglas and his great address at Cooper Union in New York City brought him into national prominence. He was elected to the presidency in 1860 and reelected in 1864.

With moving eloquence, untiring perseverance, and abounding patience, he gave himself to the preservation of the Union through four years of terrible and fratricidal war.

In his introduction to *Lincoln Talks,* a biography in anecdote, Emanuel Hertz made the statement that Lincoln was a mighty tree and that the shade he cast will endure as long as there is an American history. Incidentally, neither William E. Barton nor Carl Sandburg gives one the feeling that Lincoln is revealed and understood as does Hertz in the 672 pages of *Lincoln Talks.* Albert J. Beveridge, who died in 1927, completed the first part of a life of Lincoln which gave promise of being the most definitive and authoritative of the many biographies of President Lincoln. It covered his life up to his inauguration; I have a feeling that had Beveridge lived to complete the work, much light would have been shed where it is most needed.

Lincoln was a lonely man. In the counsels of war, in the meetings of his cabinet, and in his own home, he walked alone.

Faults he had, to be sure; but, after making every discount for his faults, the student of Lincoln's life is always astonished by the sum total of his greatness.

The tragedy of Lincoln's assassination on April 14, 1865, shocked the South no less than the North and opened the gates for a saturnalia of violence and hatred which to this day has its baleful effect upon our nation.

While President Lincoln did not belong to any church, it is generally conceded that he was a Christian and that he found in the Bible and in prayer guidance and strength for the heavy burdens of his private and presidential responsibilities.

It might well have been Lincoln about whom Matthew Arnold wrote:

> The epoch ends, the world is still.
> The age has talk'd and work'd its fill—
>
> . . . .
>
> And in the after-silence sweet,
> Now strifes are hush'd, our ear doth meet,
> Ascending pure, the bell-like fame
> Of this or that down-trodden name.
>
> . . . .
>
> And o'er that wide plain, now wrapt in gloom,
> Where many a splendor finds its tomb,
> Many spent fames and fallen mights—
> The one or two immortal lights
> Rise slowly up into the sky
> To shine there everlastingly.

The Voice of the Altar

When Lincoln took the oath of office for his second term as President, he had led the Union through four years of a war in which the blood of thousands of men soaked the earth. Scarcely more than a month after the inauguration, his own blood was to ebb out as he sat in a box at Ford's Theater.

The sixteenth chapter of Revelation, from which Lincoln selected his inaugural text, is a chapter of blood, the chapter in which the seven bowls of the wrath of God are poured out upon the earth in appalling sequence. In the midst of the emptying of God's wrath, the voice of the altar is heard saying, "Yea, O Lord God, the Almighty, true and righteous are thy judgments"—the words that Lincoln pressed to his lips on March 4, 1865.

Could it have been with a flash of insight such as is frequently granted to men not far from death, that on that March day he saw in these words a truth obscured from most men by passion and hatred? For no sooner was he dead than the words he had so bravely and eloquently spoken at Gettysburg were scorned by Thad Stevens and his ilk.

How correct *it is* that only the judgments of God are true and righteous! Because such judgments must be based on complete knowledge of men and of events, of action and of intent, of circumstance and of courage, of ability and of purpose, men can never give them. At best, men know only in part, and see through a glass darkly. It is impossible for them to be free from bias and prejudice.

God never pronounces his judgments in a spirit of querulousness. Nor does he compromise or condone. Read Ezekiel 18:20-28, or Matthew 25, or the majestic strophes of Revelation 20:11-15. And when you have done so, listen to the echo in your own heart: "Yea, O Lord God, the Almighty, true and righteous are thy judgments."

God's judgments reveal the depths of man's depravity. Even the altar itself came into being because of the wickedness of men. We read that, following the flood and the abatement of the waters, Noah built an altar and offered thereon burnt offerings, the clean for the unclean. From its very inception, the altar was a symbol of the judgment of sinful men by a holy God. It is no wonder, then, that John recorded the altar as declaring that the judgments of God are true and righteous.

Without judgment Christianity would be a contradiction, good and evil growing alongside each other in continued acquiesence. Well does Denny strike at this impossible status quo: "The dualistic conception of an endless suspense, in which good and evil permanently balance each other and contest with each other the right to inherit the earth, is virtually atheistic and the whole Bible is a protest against it." He might well have added that the whole course of human history is against it.

Saith the Scriptures: "We must all be made manifest before the judgment-seat of Christ; that each one may receive the things done in the body, according to what he hath done, whether it be good or bad" (2 Corinthians 5:10). It has been said that because men have made material things supreme, the effects of judgment are first seen in the realm of the material, or physical.

[6]

In *Hamlet* the king, guilty of the murder of his brother, cried:

> In the corrupted currents of this world
> Offence's gilded hand may shove by justice,
> . . . .
> . . . But 'tis not so above;
> There is no shuffling, there the action lies
> In his true nature; and we ourselves compell'd,
> Even to the teeth and forehead of our faults,
> To give in evidence.

If the tragic unfolding of mankind's story has any unmistakable verdict, it is that sin must be punished. What hope then is there for mankind? "For all have sinned and fall short of the glory of God" (Romans 3:23). Is that where we are to be left, bereft and undone?

Listen to Paul on Mars' Hill:

> The times of ignorance therefore God overlooked; but now he commandeth men that they should all everywhere repent: inasmuch as he hath appointed a day in which he will judge the world in righteousness by the man whom he hath ordained; wherefore he hath given assurance unto all men, in that he hath raised him from the dead (Acts 17:30-31).

One of the mighty meanings of Calvary is that there mercy and truth were met together, and righteousness and peace did kiss each other.

> Wherefore it behooved him in all things to be made like unto his brethren, that he might become a merciful and faithful high priest in things pertaining to God, to make propitiation for the sins of the people. . . . Having then a great high priest, who hath passed through the heavens, Jesus the Son of God, let us hold fast our confession. For we have not a high priest that cannot be touched with the feeling of our infirmities; but one that hath been in all points tempted like as we are, yet without sin. Let us therefore draw near with boldness unto the throne of grace, that we may receive mercy, and may find grace to help us in the time of need. . . . Inasmuch as it is appointed unto men once to die, and after this cometh judgment; so Christ also, having been once offered to bear the sins of

many, shall appear a second time, apart from sin, to them that wait for him, unto salvation (Hebrews 2:17; 4:14-16; 9:27-28).

Because thus, in the infinite wisdom and love of God, Christ died for our sins, the just for the unjust, you and I can say:

There is therefore now no condemnation to them that are in Christ Jesus. . . . If God is for us, who is against us? He that spared not his own Son, but delivered him up for us all, how shall he not also with him freely give us all things?. . . Nay, in all these things we are more than conquerors through him that loved us (Romans 8:1, 31-32, 37).

Andrew Johnson

President

April 15, 1865—March 4, 1869

Ezekiel 11:21

But as for them whose heart walketh after the heart of their detestable things and their abominations, I will bring their way upon their own heads, saith the Lord Jehovah.

Andrew Johnson

Andrew Johnson

Born December 29, 1808, Raleigh, North Carolina.
Died July 31, 1875, Carters Station, Tennessee.

An orphan at an early age, he became a tailor's apprentice at the age of ten. He moved to Greeneville, Tennessee, when he was eighteen.

So far as formal schooling went, he had none. In rapid succession he became mayor of Greeneville, a member of the Tennessee legislature, a member of Congress, governor of Tennessee, vice-president of the United States, and, on the death of Lincoln, the seventeenth President.

The radicals, such as Winter Davis and Ben Wade, who hated Lincoln's policies for the healing of our national wounds, felt that Johnson would fall in with their plans. It is said that when Wade heard that Johnson had chosen the text, "But as for them whose heart walketh after the heart of their detestable things and their abominations, I will bring their way upon their own heads," he rubbed his hands in glee and said, "This means the end of the Sodomites of the South." History records how poor indeed was Ben Wade's ability as an expositor and as a judge of men.

Articles of impeachment were drawn up against Johnson, and language was exhausted to excoriate him. By one vote only did he escape removal from office.

Following four stormy years in the White House, he went back to his home in Greeneville. Seven years later he returned to Washington as a senator from Tennessee and assumed office in the chamber where he had heard the cruel slanders of Thad Stevens. He was the first ex-president to come back to the Senate.

Two years before his death, during the summer recess of Congress in 1875, Johnson had said, while in a grave illness, "I have performed my duty to my God, my country, and my family. Approaching death is to me the mere shadow of God's protecting wing," which shadow became a reality on July 31, 1875.

So he passed over the river and laid him down in the shade of the tree whose "leaves were for the healing of the nations." For the preservation of his nation's orderly, constitutional proceedings he had done so much. Calumny could not hurt him any more; done were grief and war.

For sixty years the figure of this man was shadowed by bitterness and misunderstanding. Largely because of the monumental work of Lloyd Paul Stryker, published in 1929, entitled *Andrew Johnson,* we realize the terrible ordeal of hatred through which he passed. Congressman Andrew Jackson Montague, a former governor of Virginia and a member of our Grove Avenue Baptist Church in Richmond, once said to me, "Pastor, Stryker has rescued Johnson from oblivion."

Johnson was a member of the Methodist Church.

Retribution, Renovation, and Restoration

Ezekiel was a priest in the Temple at Jerusalem, and was carried to Babylon by Nebuchadnezzar about 597 B. C., before the rebellion of Zedekiah and the destruction of Jerusalem by Nebuchadnezzar. While a captive in the Hebrew colony on the banks of the Chebar, a small stream flowing into the Euphrates, Ezekiel had his visions and gave to the people the messages recorded in the book that bears his name.

The book of Ezekiel is one of the most difficult books in the Bible to understand. Jerome called it "the ocean of Scriptures and the labyrinth of the mysteries of God." We are told that the Jews had a law that no one could read it until thirty years of age.

Like all difficult books, it contains marvelous treasures of truth for anyone who will give his heart to the searching. Whatever the extent of the book's mystery, no one can read it without having registered on his heart the profound fact that there is a God who holds the reins in his hands.

The prevailing conviction of the leaders of Israel was that Jehovah had forsaken the land. The prophet's answer was that this conviction was true and that the cause of God's averted face was their practice of idolatry, but that, though God had ceased to dwell among his people, he had not waived his power nor his will to punish them for their sins. This is the chief message contained in chapter 11, from which Andrew Johnson chose his inaugural verse.

The conviction of having been forsaken by Jehovah had had two results: It had led to the multiplication of idols to take Jehovah's place. And it had brought into being a reckless and active resistance to Jehovah, somewhat in the spirit of, having already lost everything which Jehovah can give, we have nothing to lose; and we may gain in the material world, that being all that there is left to fight for.

"Syncretism in religion," said John Skinner, "and fatalism in politics, these are the twin symptoms of the decay of faith among the upper classes in the Jerusalem remnant."

The late G. Campbell Morgan, speaking of Ezekiel, said that his vision was characterized by penetration and that perhaps the word "through" best describes the quality of his prophecy. His messages were addressed originally to the exiles in capitivity; and yet it is evident that *through* them he spoke to all Israel. Moreover, Dr. Morgan went on to say, "Ezekiel distinctly affirmed, in the course of his prophecy, that the application of the truths he enunciated is for all men." He not only spoke *through* the exiles to Israel, but *through* Israel to all men of all nationalities and of all time.

> A man that looks on glass
> On it may stay his eye;
> Or if he pleaseth through it pass,
> And thus the heavens espy.

There are in Ezekiel many passages of almost frenzied beauty and of soaring reaches and stupendous power, which leave one breathless with awe. There is also in the book a quality that leaves one wondering, after each reading, if the interpretation he has come to accept might not be far short of what Ezekiel actually meant. I have a feeling of kinship with a friend who says that Ezekiel is more difficult to understand than Browning.

We will readily acknowledge that the love of God is too great for us to understand, because it is infinite. Yet, though we are amazed by it, we can believe it. And at the heart of all the prophecy of Ezekiel is the yearning of God for the wayward. Retribution is lost in God's renovation. "As I live, saith the Lord God, I have no pleasure in the death of the wicked; but that the wicked turn from his way and live: turn ye, turn ye from your evil ways; for why will ye die, O house of Israel?" (Ezekiel 33:11 KJV).

When judgment should have wrought its purpose and the repentant should be ready to serve God again, then would Jehovah's face be turned toward them in mercy, declared Ezekiel. In the verses just preceding the verse on which the lips of Andrew Johnson rested, there is the statement by which the entire prophecy is to be interpreted. When the people shall have repented, as he has longed for them to do, then, says God:

> I will give them one heart, and I will put a new spirit within you; and I will take the stony heart out of their flesh, and will give them an heart of flesh: that they may walk in my statutes, and keep mine ordinances, and do them: and they shall be my people, and I will be their God (Ezekiel 11:19-20 KJV).

Almost the same words are found in Ezekiel 36:26.

There must be a "within" before there can be a "without"! The glory of Christ must be an inner possession if there is to be any validity in an outward profession.

> And ah for a man to arise in me,
> That the man I am may cease to be!
> —TENNYSON

It might as truthfully be said, "The man I am must cease to be before the Man of God can reside in me."

Though Ezekiel may not have known how God would consummate the restoration of a people whose sins had brought about such a retribution of disaster as that which had befallen Israel, he was given the vision to look beyond and see a throne and on that throne a Man. I doubt that he knew what we know about the incarnation of that blessed hope. But whatever the trial, whatever the suffering, he kept the hope ever before him and lifted up his voice in a constant refrain: "The Lord is there."

Even in the just retribution of Ezekiel 11:21, "But as for them whose heart walketh after the heart of their detestable things and their abominations, I will bring their way upon their own heads," God goes on to say that it may be that they will reconsider.

Reverently and in truth it can be said that this is what God lives for, that sinful men may reconsider. That is why Christ came; that was the reason for his tears over Jerusalem.

Ulysses S. Grant

President

March 4, 1869—March 4, 1877

Isaiah 11:1

And there shall come forth a shoot out of the stock of Jesse, and a branch out of his roots shall bear fruit.

U. S. Grant

Ulysses Simpson Grant

Born April 27, 1822, Point Pleasant, Ohio.
Died July 23, 1885, Mount McGregor, New York.

The eighteenth President of the United States, the first child of Jesse and Hannah Simpson Grant, was born in a humble two-room house.

For six weeks he was without a name, and then the name Ulysses was the result of lot. The story is that following an argument as to what the child should be called, the assembled relatives each wrote a name on a slip of paper, and then one was drawn. It was Ulysses, the name proposed by his Grandmother Simpson. Then someone tacked on the name Hiram in front of Ulysses.

It was not until Grant went to West Point that the name by which he is known to the world was given him, that, too, by accident. The congressman who proposed him for West Point thought that the name by which he was always called, Ulysses, was the only one he had and, thinking that he should have a middle name, added thereto Simpson, his mother's family name. Thus was given to the world U. S. Grant.

Following his graduation from West Point, twenty-first in a class of thirty-nine, he saw service in the Mexican War. Resigning from the army, he entered business, in which he was far from fortunate. At the beginning of the War Between the States, he re-entered the army; and by his dogged persistence and courage, rather than brilliance of command, he brought about the surrender of Lee's army at Appomattox, April 9, 1865, which for all intents and purposes ended the war.

He served two terms as President. The verse he pressed to his lips on his first inauguration day, March 4, 1869, was Isaiah 11:1, "And there shall come forth a shoot out of the stock of Jesse, and a branch out of his roots shall bear fruit." There is irony in this; for, bear in mind, his father's name was Jesse.

Who can tell what motivated him to choose that verse? Or was it chosen for him? Certainly the fruit which his administration bore was bitter indeed, apples of ashes. Not until Harding's was there to be another administration to compare with his in political debauchery; and bad as was Harding's, it was pale compared to the blackness of Grant's. Personally honest, he was as a child in the hands of the skilful crooks who surrounded him and who succeeded in destroying a large part of the effectiveness of his own undoubtedly high purpose. On that sordid chapter, let history cast a mantle of oblivion.

Shortly before his death he wrote a letter to his wife and put it in his pocket.

Look after our dear children and direct them in the paths of rectitude. It would distress me far more to hear that one of them could depart from an honorable, upright and virtuous life than it would to know that they were prostrated on a bed of sickness from which they were never to arise alive. They have never given us any cause for alarm on this account, and I trust they never will. With these few injunctions and the knowledge I have of your love and affection and the dutiful affection of all our children, I bid you a final farewell, until we meet in another, and I trust, better world. You will find this on my person after my demise.

There is tragedy, compounded tragedy, revealed in that letter. "Direct them in the paths of rectitude"! How the dying man must have travailed in the memory of the dishonesty and fraud which had blackened his administration.

Grant's courage was never shown more gallantly than when, ravaged by a malignant disease, he set about writing his memoirs in order to pay off his debts and provide for his family.

The *Christian Statesman* reported, "It is not on record that he spoke at any time of the Savior, or expressed his sense of dependence on His atonement and mediation." Nevertheless, Grant was not an atheist; he believed in God and hoped for a better life, as his letter to his wife reveals.

He attended the services of the Methodist Church with Mrs. Grant, although on the authority of W. E. Woodard, he never became a member of the church.

The Son of Jesse

From his vision to the very end of his book, the prophet Isaiah exalts the sovereignty of God—a throne veiled, a throne unveiled, and, most significant of all, a throne occupied.

The grandeur of the book of Isaiah is its revelation of the abiding throne and its Occupant, whose purpose for all mankind is so movingly and powerfully set forth in the beloved fifty-third chapter. That Occupant was "out of the stock of Jesse."

Matthew began his genealogy of Jesus with three names—Jesus, David, Abraham. In verses 5 and 6 of chapter 1, he said, "Obed begat Jesse, and Jesse begat David the king."

Luke, in his genealogy of our Lord, chapter 3, verses 31 and 32, said, "Nathan the son of David, the son of Jesse."

Paul, in Acts 13:21-23, speaking in the synagogue in Antioch of Psidia, declared:

And afterward they asked for a king: and God gave unto them Saul the son of Kish, a man of the tribe of Benjamin, for the space of forty years. And when he had removed him, he raised up David to be their king; to whom also he bare witness and said, I have found David the son of Jesse, a man after my heart, who shall do all my will. Of this man's seed hath God according to promise brought unto Israel a Saviour, Jesus.

Lest there be any remaining doubt as to whom the verse chosen by President Grant refers, Isaiah 11:10 is quoted in Romans 15:12, "There shall be the root of Jesse, and he that ariseth to rule over the Gentiles; on him shall the Gentiles hope."

So much for the establishment of the identity of Jesus as the son, the branch, of Jesse.

Not long since, I walked to Westminster Abbey at the time of evensong. In the dimness of that historic sanctuary, I heard a voice reading from the Scriptures:

> At that time ye were without Christ, being aliens from the commonwealth of Israel, and strangers from the covenants of promise, having no hope, and without God in the world. . . . For he is our peace, who hath made both one, and hath broken down the middle wall of partition between us . . . that he might reconcile both unto God in one body by the cross (Ephesians 2:12-16 KJV).

The late sunlight was shining on the altar and tipped the high golden cross with the redness of its rays.

It was a strange and, at first thought, irrelevant commentary on the bomb-pocked city, so recently bathed in the bitter brew of men's hatred for each other. Aliens from each other! A wall of partition between! Is that the destiny of man? And then I saw again the blood-red tip of the cross—God's opinion of man and the world. "For it was the good pleasure of the Father that . . . through him to reconcile all things unto himself, having made peace through the blood of his cross" (Colossians 1:19-20).

But what of the fruits of this branch of Jesse? It is two thousand years since Christ died. Let no man, looking at this sad and sinful world, a world full of multiform bewilderment, say that of fruit there is little evidence—though far too little fruit there is, we can but admit.

Why so little fruit? We must keep firmly fixed in our thinking the gulf between the adequacy of the cross and the inadequacy of man's response to the call of the cross. There is within each of us who wears the name of Christian the lack of a confident, virile, and victorious faith in the fact that God in Christ claims the world. There is in that claim a stark realism that we have not grasped. It demands a willingness to acknowledge in action the passion and the consecration of Christ.

Cecil Northcutt has well said, "There is no immediate victory offered, nor is the battle brief." But the final triumph of the living Christ is assured in the eternal purpose of Almighty God, whose Son he is.

"Do you think He is dead?" asked Pilate's wife, in Masefield's *Trial of Jesus*.

"No, lady, I don't," replied the centurion.

"Then where is He?"

"Let loose in the world, lady, where neither Roman nor Jew can stop His truth."

Rutherford B. Hayes

President

March 5, 1877—March 4, 1881

Psalm 118:11-13

They compassed me about; yea, they compassed me about:
In the name of Jehovah I will cut them off.
They compassed me about like bees; they are quenched as the fire
  of thorns:
In the name of Jehovah I will cut them off.
Thou didst thrust sore at me that I might fall;
But Jehovah helped me.

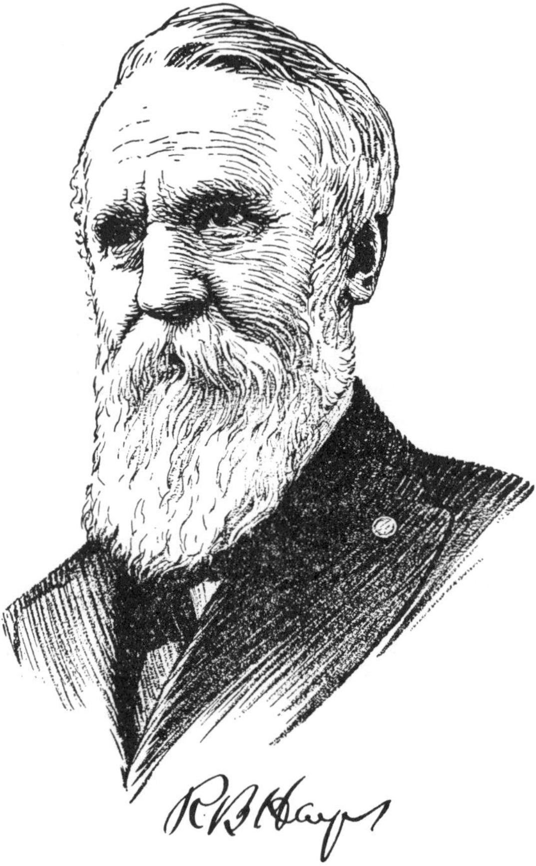

Rutherford Birchard Hayes

Born October 4, 1822, Delaware, Ohio.
Died January 17, 1893, Fremont, Ohio.

Our nineteenth President was born after the death of his father; but through the financial aid of an uncle, he received a good education, graduating from Kenyon College. He became a lawyer, and affiliated with the newly born Republican party upon its merger with the old Whig party.

He served as a brigadier general in the Union Army, as a member of Congress from Ohio, and as governor of Ohio for three terms. He was his party's candidate for President against Samuel J. Tilden. That campaign produced an amazing paradox: Hayes, the man who became President, was not elected. The election was thrown into the hands of a commission of fifteen, and by a vote of eight to seven, they cast all the disputed electoral votes for Hayes, making the final figures 185 to 184. For all the shouting and all the cries of fraud, the country was better off than it would have been if Tilden had been elected.

Hayes was fifty-four years old when he was inaugurated President on March 5, 1877. He upheld the Constitution, removed the bayonets and the carpetbag governments from the South, and gave the South a chance to live. There were no scandals in his official family, and political scalawags were exterminated. With the Hayes administration, what Don Carlos Seitz called "the dreadful decade" came to an end.

To be sure, there were those who sneered at the simple life of this good man and his lovely wife. One of the objects of scorn and subjects of derision was his executive order against the sale of intoxicating liquors as a beverage at the camps, forts, and other posts of the army. The entire absence of intoxicating liquors from the White House gave William H. Evarts, Hayes's secretary of state, the opportunity to observe that "water flowed like champagne in the White House."

Hayes attended the Methodist Church, and for him there was reality in religion.

A Song of Deliverance

The passage of Scripture chosen by President Hayes for his inauguration is a pointed reminder of the conspiring events and political recriminations which ushered him into the presidency.

> They compassed me about; yea, they compassed me about:
> In the name of Jehovah I will cut them off.
> They compassed me about like bees; they are quenched as
>   the fire of thorns:
> In the name of Jehovah I will cut them off.
> Thou didst thrust sore at me that I might fall;
> But Jehovah helped me.

In John Hill Burton's *History of Scotland* there is this story about John Knox when he was serving as a slave on board a French galley:

> His galley-companion, James Balfour, asked "if he thought that ever they should be delivered;" to which Knox answered, "that God would deliver them from that bondage to His glory even in this life." Soon after this their galley coasted Scotland, passing familiar spots. They were tossing in the Bay of St. Andrews, where Knox was so reduced by sickness that "few hoped for his life," when his companion, turning to him, "willed him to look at the land, and asked him if he knew it;" who answered "Yes, I know it well; for I see the steeple of that place where God first in public opened my mouth to His glory; and I am fully persuaded, how weak that ever I now appear, that I shall not depart this life till that my tongue shall glorify His godly name in that same place."

Psalm 118 is one of jubilant praise for rescue from peril, bondage, and persecution; it is a song of the redeemed; it is a jubilate for the deliverance wrought by the almighty hand of a sovereign God. One note is continually emphasized:

Jehovah answered me.... Jehovah is on my side.... It is better to take refuge in Jehovah than to put confidence in man.... In the name of Jehovah I will cut them off.... Jehovah helped me. Jehovah is my strength and song; and he is become my salvation.... The right hand of Jehovah doeth valiantly.... This is Jehovah's doing.

How oft repeated is this glad acknowledgment of the sovereignty of God and his power to deliver!

Without a realization of the sovereignty of God, we are in danger of falling into the torpor of fatalism, an impossible substitute for a triumphant faith in the purposes, power, and preeminence of God. God is sovereign; he cannot be finally thwarted; he will make even the wrath of men to praise him. Without limitation is he, but how limited are we!

In my young manhood I helped build the railroad from Frannie, Wyoming, to Worland, Wyoming. The track was laid on a line which had been plotted and designated by the surveyors. On each side of the track, at indicated locations, were spurs for sidetracks, divergences from the main line. These sidetracks were limited and were not to be confused with the main direction.

We may think of the purposes of God in somewhat the same way. The main line of God's will has been laid down. And though men may shape their way in the light of their own ambitions, they cannot move beyond God's will for them without coming to disaster. This Israel discovered; this all men must discover.

However, God can use even disasters for his ultimate victory, and he can make the results of sin an instrument of discipline and a means of redemption. The marvel is that thinking men will either ignore or defy the beneficent sovereignty of God, which is bent to their own best interests.

Luther's hymn *"Ein feste Burg ist unser Gott"* has its background in this thought: "Jehovah is my strength and song, and he is become my salvation." A more moving hymn of faith and trust there is none.

President Hayes was one of our presidents who firmly held to the conviction, "Thou art my God, and I will give thanks unto thee; thou art my God, I will exalt thee." In *Messages and Papers of the Presidents,* under date of October 29, 1877, are these words from Hayes:

> Under a sense of these infinite obligations to the Great Ruler of Times and Seasons and Events, let us humbly ascribe it to our own faults and frailties if in any degree that perfect concord and happiness, peace and justice, which such great mercies should diffuse through the hearts and lives of our people do not altogether and always and everywhere prevail.

Years ago an anonymous English poet sang:

> Through men's chaos a higher Power discerns
> The pattern of the Whole, nor from its aim
> Is Time deflected. Therefore let none claim
> That man's despite aeonian ruin earns.
>
> Unapprehended some almighty Hand
> Or rules, or overrules. Not ours to see
> The ordered obverse of the tapestry
> By human history wrought, nor understand
>
> By proof or vision that beyond the strand
> Of time an ultimate Theodicy,
> A consummation and a Rest shall be,
> For that which Love engendered, Wisdom planned.

Whoever the poet was, he had keen insight into the truths of God's sovereignty.

> They compassed me about; yea, they compassed me about:
> In the name of Jehovah I will cut them off.
> They compassed me about like bees; they are quenched as the fire of thorns:
> In the name of Jehovah I will cut them off.

The voice of rejoicing and salvation is in the tents of the righteous:
The right hand of Jehovah doeth valiantly.

Let us be sure of this: the one fact is God; all other things are circumstances.

Rightly considered, could not the parable which we call "the prodigal son" as truly be called the parable of "the loving father"? Oh, how long had that father waited for the lad to come to himself! And the son had to come to himself before he could come to his father. And how farsighted was that father! He saw the weary figure long before he stumbled into his arms and began —begin is all he ever did—to make his confession. How beautifully illustrative of the loving sovereignty of our blessed Lord is this story!

One day we shall all stand looking over the river. One day, like Stonewall Jackson, we shall all ask that someone shall pick us up and gently lay us down in the shade of the trees. Then will the sovereignty of God become for us, not just a matter of theology in which we implicitly believe but now know only in part; it will be a glorious revelation of a mighty fact.

James A. Garfield

President

March 4, 1881—September 19, 1881

Proverbs 21:1

The king's heart is in the hand of Jehovah as the watercourses:
He turneth it whithersoever he will.

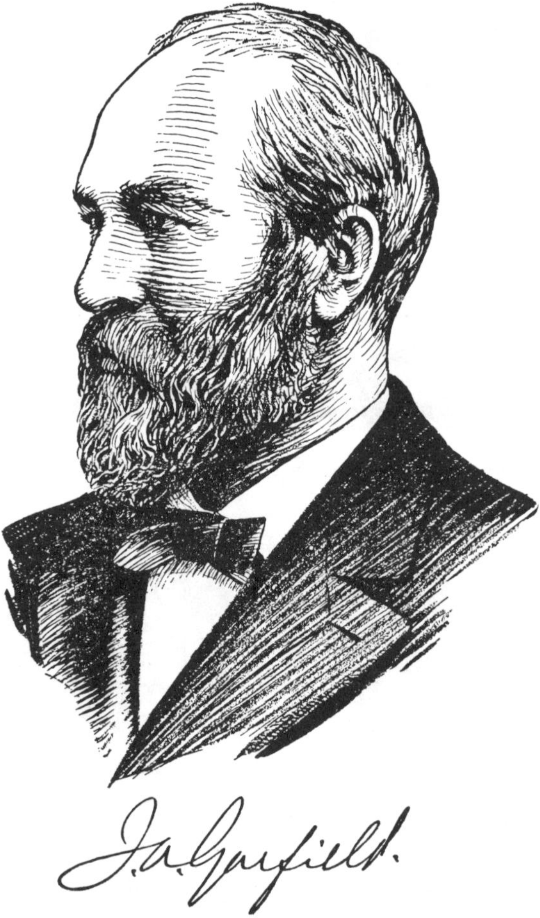
J.A. Garfield.

JAMES ABRAM GARFIELD

Born November 19, 1831, Orange, Ohio.
Died September 19, 1881, Elberon, New Jersey.

Garfield, the twentieth President of the United States, was born in a log cabin. He was of New England stock, his parents having moved in 1830 from Connecticut to what was then known as the Western Reserve.

His father died at the age of thirty-three, leaving his widow with four small children, of whom James was the youngest. At the age of ten James Garfield was already accustomed to manual labor. He learned and practiced the trade of a carpenter. By stern physical discipline and strict mental application, he completed the work offered at the district school; attended Hiram College, of which he afterward became president; and graduated with honor from Williams College. He was admitted to the bar in 1859.

He was converted under the ministry of a Disciples of Christ minister, and united with that church and frequently served as a lay preacher.

During the War Between the States, he rose from the command of a regiment, the Forty-second Ohio Volunteers, to the rank of major general.

For eight successive terms he was elected to the House of Representatives. He was elected to the Senate; but before he could take his seat, he was nominated for the presidency by the Republican party at the Chicago convention, where he had opposed Grant's candidacy for a third term.

He was inaugurated as President on March 4, 1881. On July 2, 1881, he was shot by an assassin in the Baltimore and Ohio Railroad Station in Washington, D. C., and never recovered from the effects of the wound. His death took place at Elberon, New Jersey, at 10:30 P. M., September 19, 1881. He was President but six and a half months. Only one of our Presidents, William Henry Harrison, served a shorter time.

President Garfield's assassin was Charles Guiteau, a lawyer, whose mind had become inflamed by the bitter campaign preceding the election. It is significant that each of our three Presidents who were assassinated was shot by a man whose mind had broken under the violence of political events.

Thy Will Be Done

The verse President Garfield chose for his inaugural text was Proverbs 21:1:

> The king's heart is in the hand of Jehovah as the watercourses:
> He turneth it whithersoever he will.

In one of our older hymns, this thought of trust in Jehovah is beautifully set forth:

> "My times are in Thy hand";
> My God, I wish them there;
> My life, my friends, my soul, I leave
> Entirely to Thy care.
>
> "My times are in Thy hand";
> Whatever they may be;
> Pleasing or painful, dark or bright,
> As best may seem to Thee.
> —WILLIAM F. LOYD

We are accustomed to speak of the books of Job, Proverbs, and Ecclesiastes as books of wisdom, meaning, not that there is a lack of wisdom in the other books of the Bible, but that the viewpoint of these three is philosophical.

It should be kept in mind when reading Proverbs that its philosophy is based upon an affirmation—an affirmation of the wisdom and power of God and of his concern for mankind. The great philosophers of the world—Plato and Aristotle, to name but two of the most familiar—do not start with a premise of God's power; instead, they begin by asking whether there be a God. The Hebrew philosophers begin with God and move out into the world of thought; Plato and the moderns who follow in his train begin out in the world of thought and move in, searching for God—if there be such.

Proverbs 9:10 puts it this way: "The fear of Jehovah is the beginning of wisdom." By "fear" is not meant dread—that would be to cringe; by "fear" is meant love, and that is to worship.

To view life in any way other than with faith in, and fear of, God is to apply but a limited human therapy to the problems of life, an ineffectual palliative. How can we phrase this truth so that men, with all their disappointments and defeats, shall have their hope rekindled, and so that their hearts shall know peace? In this inaugural verse of President Garfield is the answer, hidden but discoverable:

> The king's heart is in the hand of Jehovah as the watercourses:
> He turneth it whithersoever he will.

This verse does not convey the meaning that kings, nor commoners, dangle at the ends of strings held in the relentless hand of Omnipotence. That would be to make of those created in the image of God mere puppets, passive tools in the directive will of an unloving destiny. Many people have sunk into this view; for them "the struggle naught availeth." But such an interpretation is a perversion of the truth, a travesty on the very nature of God and on his loving purpose.

One word explains the teaching of this verse, and that word is "submission." Jehovah does not seize the resisting heart of the king and hold it in a ruthless grasp. The king places his heart in the hand of Jehovah; then, in glad submission, he becomes usable for whatever purpose God sees as best.

To say that God does not seize our hearts is not to deny God's right to command our lives; that right, as all rights, belongs to him and cannot be abrogated. The way of submission is a higher way than the way of compulsion, unless, of course, we make the compulsion of love to take precedence.

This verse points to the profound truth that to yield is to gain. Jesus spoke much of this. He insisted that unless "a corn of wheat fall in the ground and die, it abideth alone." He expressed this truth in his death on the cross, when his enemies railed on him and shouted, "He saved others; himself he cannot save." As someone has suggested, it was not that he was not able to save himself, but rather that he was able not to save himself and so is able to save to the uttermost all who come to God through him.

All this was previewed in the prayer in the garden of Gethsemane: "Father, if thou be willing, remove this cup from me: nevertheless not my will, but thine, be done." There is not a trace of weakness in such submission as this. Nor is there aught of recrimination or complaint. This is strength personified. In Christ were embodied what Paul describes with such amazing exactness in the second chapter of Philippians, verses 5-11: condescension, descension, ascension.

Only as we are willing to say, "Not my will, but thine," and mean it, are we usable; and only as we are usable, do we find the reality of happiness. In "Locksley Hall Sixty Years After," Tennyson comments on this truth thus:

What are men that He should heed us? cried the king of sacred song;
Insects of an hour, that hourly work their brother insect wrong?

. . . .

Only That which made us, meant us to be mightier by and by,
Set the sphere of all the boundless Heavens within the human eye,

Sent the shadow of Himself, the boundless, thro' the human soul;
Boundless inward, in the atom, boundless outward in the Whole.

Surprisingly few have been the kings who have placed their hearts in submission to the purposes of Jehovah; and just as surprisingly few have been the commoners. I say "surprisingly,"

[39]

because the concerted evidence of the ages would compel the acknowledgment that without such submission there is to be found neither success nor happiness. No wonder the psalmist prayed that his soul, which he said "cleaveth unto the dust," should be given life by God's Word! Without the submission of our hearts to the will of Jehovah, we live but in a lingering death.

The man who places his heart in the hand of Jehovah
>   . . . shall be like a tree planted by the streams of water,
>   That bringeth forth its fruit in its season,
>   Whose leaf also doth not wither;
>   And whatsoever he doeth shall prosper.

This is the portrait of a happy man—happy because his delight is to do the will of Jehovah, happy because he has said with a recognizing submission, *"Thy* will be done."

But such submission is not natural for us, and does not come easily. For our will is not, by nature, to do the will of God. Our "won'ts" contradict the will of God.

Chester A. Arthur

President

September 20, 1881—March 4, 1885

Psalm 31:1-3

In thee, O Jehovah, do I take refuge;
Let me never be put to shame:
Deliver me in thy righteousness.
Bow down thine ear unto me; deliver me speedily:
Be thou to me a strong rock,
A house of defence to save me.
For thou art my rock and my fortress;
Therefore for thy name's sake lead me and guide me.

Charles H. Filkins

CHESTER ALAN ARTHUR

Born October 5, 1830, Fairfield, Vermont.
Died November 18, 1886, New York, New York.

Chester Alan Arthur, our twenty-first President, was the eldest son of Rev. William Arthur and Malvina Stone Arthur. His father, a Baptist preacher, was born in Ireland.

Arthur was graduated from Union College at the age of eighteen, sixth in a class of one hundred. He studied law, and in 1853 was admitted to the bar and became a member of the law firm of Culver, Parker, and Arthur in New York City.

His military career was confined to noncombat duty. In 1862 he was appointed inspector general of New York troops, and later he was appointed quartermaster general of New York, with the rank of brigadier general. He retired from the army on December 31, 1862, and engaged in law practice until President Grant appointed him as collector of the port of New York, one of the most lucrative posts in appointive power. He held this office until he was suspended by President Hayes, July 11, 1878.

He had been an ardent advocate of Grant to succeed Hayes. When Garfield was nominated for the presidency, it seemed wise to have a "Grant man" for his running mate, and Arthur was accordingly made the nominee for vice-president.

On the death of Garfield, Arthur became President, taking the oath of office on September 20, 1881, at his residence in New York City. On September 22, the oath of office was formally administered by Chief Justice Waite in the vice-president's room in the Capitol.

Arthur died suddenly at his residence in New York City, November 18, 1886, and was buried at Albany.

History has not been too kind to Arthur's achievements as President, but it is due him to say that he rose much higher in his conduct of that office than his political affiliations would have indicated.

He was a nominal member of the Episcopal Church.

For Thy Name's Sake

In his inaugural address on September 22, 1881, President Arthur said:

> For the fourth time in the history of the Republic its Chief Magistrate has been removed by death. All hearts are filled with grief and horror at the hideous crime which has darkened our land, and the memory of the murdered President, his protracted sufferings, his unyielding fortitude, the example and achievements of his life, and the pathos of his death will forever illumine the pages of our history.
>
> For the fourth time the officer elected by the people and ordained by the Constitution to fill a vacancy so created is called to assume the Executive chair.

It was a dark hour, and Arthur, upon assuming the office of President, found himself caught between the Scylla and Charybdis of political acrimony and tossed in an embittered rapids of unrequited ambitions. He inherited as secretary of state James G. Blaine, who was an inveterate seeker after the presidency and who never removed his eyes from the office which he was never to fill. Students of American history will find no more intriguing study of the consequences of a struggle of individuals for power than that of the results of the rivalry between Roscoe Conkling, senator from New York, and James G. Blaine, "the plumed knight" of Maine. Each was brilliant, each was inordinately ambitious, each was venal. The assassination of Garfield can justly be traced to the hatreds growing out of the conniving and the quarrels of these two men.

Though Arthur did his best, he had constantly to deal with whirlpools of political jealousy and hatred. When, after serving out his term with a sanity and dignity unexpected by the public (which could not forget the manner in which he had conducted the office of collector of customs in New York City), he allowed his name to be presented at the Republican Convention in 1884, it was James G. Blaine who defeated him.

In the light of this situation, we can see now that the verses which Arthur chose for his inaugural text were both significant and prophetic. Well might he have said, like Banquo in *Macbeth* when he suspected the truth about Duncan's death:

> Fears and scruples shake us:
> In the great hand of God I stand; and thence
> Against the undivulg'd pretense I fight
> Of treasonous malice.

His feet were set in a larger room than any he had ever known; and as never before, he needed wisdom from above, a rock on which to stand, and a fortress in which to find security. And so he lifted the Bible to his lips and kissed these words from Psalm 31:

> In thee, O Jehovah, do I take refuge;
> Let me never be put to shame:
> Deliver me in thy righteousness.
> Bow down thine ear unto me; deliver me speedily:
> Be thou to me a strong rock,
> A house of defence to save me.
> For thou art my rock and my fortress;
> Therefore for thy name's sake lead me and guide me.

The Scottish preacher who was known as "Rabbi" Duncan once said of the angel which appeared to our Lord at Gethsemane: "If in the upper world we shall see the angel that came and ministered unto Him, I think the whole church will be interested in him." Not otherwise will it be with the author of the thirty-first Psalm, the words of which have accompanied men through their early pilgrimage and their hours of death. This psalm deals with the elemental experiences of religion and the most secret longings of the human heart.

It is the psalm of a soul in danger, but it is also the psalm of a soul whose consciousness of danger does not dim his confidence in God. Alertness to danger must not divert us from the Deliverer. If we see only our enemies and never our allies, we shall not stay long on the field of battle. But "if God be for us, who can be against us?" The realization of the only possible answer to that question will drive away our fear.

In this psalm, the psalmist perceived his danger from the intrigue of his enemies, from the deceit of his erstwhile friends, from the sin of his own heart, from the rejection of his service, and from the defaming of his character. He prayed that God would grant him deliverance in danger, grant him a shelter from hatred, in mercy blot out his iniquity, and favor him through renewed fellowship with his God.

He praised God because of his imparted strength, his implanted security, and his imputed salvation. He likened his place of divine safety to a rock, a figure that is frequently found in Psalms. Many times, as in verse 3 of Psalm 31, the word "rock" is used as a direct synonym for Jehovah, a positive designation for God. The reason for this, of course, is that a rock is the most indelible suggestion of strength and immutability. Geologists tell us that when all the flux of creation ebbed away, the rocks emerged, the ultimate in strength. To transfer the figure to the moral realm, the rock represents the victory of righteousness over wrong.

Quite easily overlooked is the principle upon which the psalmist based his plea for deliverance, as noted in the last clause of verse 3: "For thy name's sake lead me and guide me."

Daringly he stated that the honor of God was involved in this deliverance. Furthermore, he was more concerned that such honor be vindicated than he was that he should be delivered.

Such a concern is high ground indeed. Moses stood thereon when pleading for God's mercy upon a sinful and rebellious people. It is this concern which underlies the real "Lord's prayer" in John 17, and this same concern impelled Paul to declare that he could wish himself anathema from Christ for his kinsmen's sake.

Prayer thus based is certain to be answered, for it measures up to the standard of God.

Grover Cleveland

President

March 4, 1885—March 4, 1889
March 4, 1893—March 4, 1897

Psalm 112:4-10

Unto the upright there ariseth light in the darkness:
He is gracious, and merciful, and righteous.
Well is it with the man that dealeth graciously and lendeth;
He shall maintain his cause in judgment.
For he shall never be moved;
The righteous shall be had in everlasting remembrance.
He shall not be afraid of evil tidings:
His heart is fixed, trusting in Jehovah.
His heart is established, he shall not be afraid,
Until he see his desire upon his adversaries.
He hath dispersed, he hath given to the needy:
His righteousness endureth for ever:
His horn shall be exalted with honor.
The wicked shall see it, and be grieved;
He shall gnash with his teeth, and melt away:
The desire of the wicked shall perish.

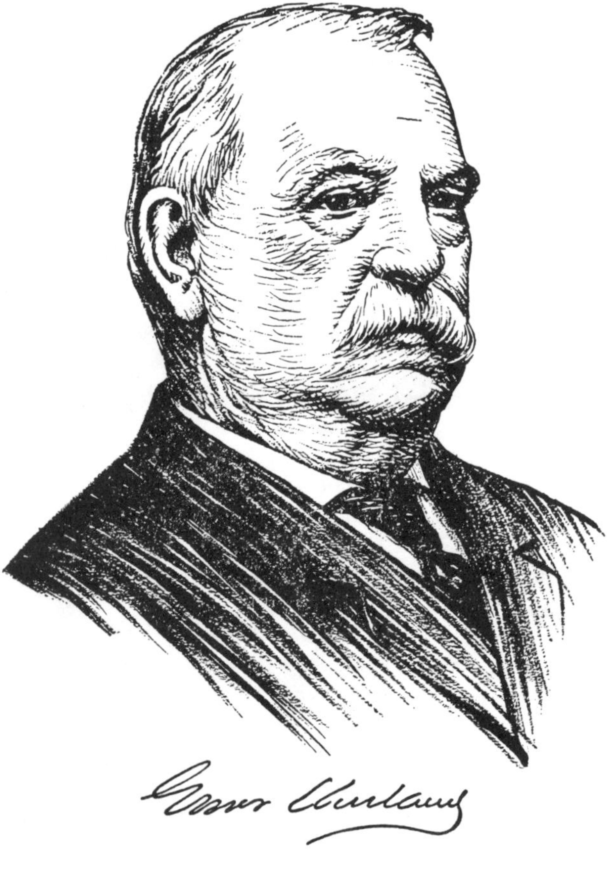

GROVER CLEVELAND

Born March 18, 1837, Caldwell, New Jersey.
Died June 24, 1908, Princeton, New Jersey.

Grover Cleveland was born in the Presbyterian parsonage at Caldwell, New Jersey, where his father was pastor. When he was four years old, his father accepted a call to the Presbyterian church at Fayetteville, New York, and there the future President attended school. When he was sixteen, his father died, and the support of his widowed mother became his responsibility. He studied law in Buffalo, New York, and was admitted to the bar in 1859. On January 1, 1863, he was appointed assistant district attorney of Erie County. He was elected on the Democratic ticket as mayor of Buffalo, entered office, January 1, 1882, and became known as fhe "veto mayor" from the use he made of the prerogative of the veto in checking unwise, illegal, and extravagant expenditures.

In 1882 he was elected governor of New York. His state administration was based on the same principles which controlled his official actions as mayor of Buffalo. He was elected President of the United States before completing his term as governor and was inaugurated, March 4, 1885.

His courage, his honesty, and his unbending adherence to what he felt to be right, brought about his defeat when he ran for a second term in the next election. But, following Benjamin Harrison's four-year term, Cleveland was again elected. Thus he was our twenty-second and our twenty-fourth President, and the only man who has served as President of our nation for two nonconsecutive terms.

President Cleveland was married in the White House on June 2, 1886, to Miss Frances Folsom, who became the youngest, except for Dolly Madison, of the first ladies of our country. She was the first wife of a President to be married in the White House and the first to give birth to a child there.

Cleveland retired from office, March 4, 1897, and went to live at Princeton. He was one of our greatest Presidents, and one of our most misunderstood. A prodigious worker, he was an untiring foe of graft and corruption wherever he found it. As a result, he was hated by many of the leaders of his own party, as well as by others.

Cleveland was a Presbyterian.

What Makes a Man?

Of Cromwell, a great historian has said, "Here was a man!" Among a host of *men,* here was a *man*. The history of England is vindication of the description. What makes a *man?* The answer is found in Psalm 112, the psalm from which President Cleveland chose the Scripture passage for his first inauguration. (For his second term, he chose Psalm 91:12-16.)

President Cleveland's first inaugural address, delivered on March 4, 1885, is not long, but it is a noble state paper which should be required reading in every course of American history in every high school in these United States. Its sentiments are lofty, and its spirit indicates the unselfish course the President was to pursue through the stormy years of his two terms. Consider a few sentences:

This impressive ceremony adds little to the solemn sense of responsibility with which I contemplate the duty I owe to all the people of the land. Nothing can relieve me from anxiety lest by any act of mine their interests may suffer, and nothing is needed to strengthen my resolution to engage every faculty and effort in the promotion of their welfare.

. . . .

At this hour the animosities of political strife, the bitterness of partisan defeat, and the exultation of partisan triumph should be supplanted by an ungrudging acquiescence in the popular will and a sober, conscientious concern for the general weal.

. . . .

In the discharge of my official duty I shall endeavor to be guided by a just and unstrained construction of the Constitution, a careful observance of the distinction between the powers granted to the Federal Government and those reserved by the States or to the people, and by a cautious appreciation of those functions which by the Constitution and laws have been especially assigned to the executive branch of the Government. . . .

. . . .

. . . It is the duty of those serving the people in public places to closely limit public expenditures to the actual needs of the Government economically administered.

. . . .

The people demand reform in the administration of the Government and the application of business principles to public affairs.

Long forgotten principles, these! And President Cleveland was a doer of the word and not a speaker only.

One segment, particularly, of his administrative policy illustrates what goes to make for greatness in the position which he occupied. During the two terms of his office, he became known as the "veto President," as he had been known as the "veto mayor." "Trough" bills and patronage-based legislation got nowhere with him, even if they meant votes for the party. He had to contend with literally hundreds of "claim" bills growing out of the War Between the States; they had short shrift from him. Raids on the public treasury found no accessory to the fact in him. Unafraid, unmoved, and unashamed, he carried out his convictions. We desperately need his kind today.

It has been suggested that Psalm 112, from which President Cleveland chose his inaugural text, is a description of a man who is right—right with God, right with himself, and right with his fellow men.

It seems strange that goodness should fail to disarm wickedness, but it never does. John Whitehead, speaking of Admiral Gaspard Coligny, said that "he impressed all, but appealed only to the few." So Paris slew him and made his dead body the object of ignoble rage. But posterity has honored him with full appreciation. "The righteous shall be had in everlasting remembrance."

What is a great man? It may at once be stated that the standards by which history has adjudged men worthy of being called great are not the standards of Psalm 112. History has conferred upon three men the accolade "the great": Alexander, Frederick, and Napoleon. And why? Only because they were conquerors by force of arms, brilliant and brutal shedders of others' blood. All three walked roughshod over the rights of others; all three grasped power as a thing for self-aggrandizement; all three inspired the cheers and plaudits of their armies; and all three died with nothing to show for their greatness but a legend, a monument, and a tomb.

What makes for greatness? Here is what the psalmist says: A man is great who fears God, whose wealth is in the affection of his home, whose hand is outstretched to help the needy, whose conduct is above reproach, whose life is as a light of guidance in a dark night, whose rectitude is always to be counted upon, whose courage is constant and contagious, and whose discharge of duty is not limited or influenced by bribery of any sort.

No one ever gave so true a definition of greatness as did our Lord: "Whoever would be great among you must be your servant, and whoever would be first among you must be slave of all. For the Son of man also came not to be served, but to serve." He was speaking to the disciples, who, like ourselves, had the idea that the mark of greatness was the possession of power.

Few men are free from the fascination of power and the temptation to yield to a desire for it. A man's real greatness is measured by the degree of his unselfishness. And the degree of a man's failure to achieve greatness is often the measure of his selfishness. One of the most tragic stories in our nation's history is that of Aaron Burr, a man who had rendered exceptional service to his country, who had expected to become President but had been by-passed. In his letters he poured out the bitterness of his soul. The sad thing is that it seems never to have occurred to him that there was anything discreditable in his thwarted ambitions.

It is love of self that gives rise to jealousy of others. And whenever our plans are crossed, it is self-esteem that makes for wounded pride, hurt sensibilities, and personal grievance.

Anyone who is on the lookout for recognition may as well adjust his sights for the lowered boom. Jesus tried to teach us this by what he said. He taught it even more by the way he lived, and that is why Paul told us that we are saved by his life. When, in the upper room, Jesus took a towel, it meant far more than taking a sword. Its effect was felt at once by the disciples: one moment before, none was willing to do that menial thing; one moment after, every man was sorry he had not done it.

Such is the effect of real greatness, and men who qualify thus shall be held in everlasting remembrance.

Benjamin Harrison

President

March 4, 1889—March 4, 1893

Psalm 121:1-6

I will lift up mine eyes unto the mountains:
From whence shall my help come?
My help cometh from Jehovah,
Who made heaven and earth.
He will not suffer thy foot to be moved:
He that keepeth thee will not slumber.
Behold, he that keepeth Israel
Will neither slumber nor sleep.
Jehovah is thy keeper:
Jehovah is thy shade upon thy right hand.
The sun shall not smite thee by day,
Nor the moon by night.

Benj Harrison

BENJAMIN HARRISON

Born August 20, 1833, North Bend, Ohio.
Died March 13, 1901, Indianapolis, Indiana.

Benjamin Harrison, the twenty-third President of the United States, was born in the home of his grandfather, William Henry Harrison, the ninth President, who lived but one month after his inauguration in 1841. He was named for his great-grandfather, Benjamin Harrison, one of the signers of the Declaration of Independence. Thus the background of our twenty-third President reaches back to the beginning of our nation's existence.

After his graduation from Miami University, Oxford, Ohio, Benjamin Harrison studied law under Storer and Gwynne in Cincinnati, and in 1854 he was admitted to the bar. He began the practice of law in Indianapolis, where he was to make his home.

When the War Between the States began, Harrison assisted in organizing the Seventieth Regiment of Indiana Volunteers, and in 1862 he became its colonel. His service was active, and before the end of the war he had been promoted to the rank of brigadier general. After the war he resumed the practice of law. From 1881 to 1887 he was United States Senator from Indiana; and when President Garfield offered him a place in his cabinet, he declined, preferring to retain his seat in the Senate.

He was nominated for the presidency in 1888 at Chicago, defeated Grover Cleveland in the election, and was inaugurated, March 4, 1889. In 1892 he was again nominated for President on the Republican ticket but was defeated by Cleveland. It has been correctly stated that President Harrison was a good man but that nothing he did gave sufficient satisfaction to insure his re-election. After his one term as President, he returned to the practice of law in Indianapolis. In 1899 he was sent to the Hague Peace Conference.

President Harrison was a Presbyterian.

Beyond the Mountains

Recalling the animosities which were aroused by the hard times that fell upon the nation during President Harrison's term of office, we can see that the choice he made of a Scripture passage, Psalm 121, for his inaugural ceremony was to the point and descriptive of his own need. Those were hard times indeed. The financial panic and the economic disasters of the early 1890's have passed into history. As we look back now, it is easy to see how foolish it was to make President Harrison chargeable for those sad days; but to the men out of work and to their families clamoring for bread, he alone was responsible.

When times are hard, the man who can keep office is he who promises everything and delivers on deficit spending. It was therefore quite natural that Benjamin Harrison, who would do neither, went from the White House after one term to resume the practice of law.

He was, as a matter of record, a good President, and there was nothing in his conduct, either during his term of office or after, that gives any indication of failure to find the inner peace and security promised in Psalm 121.

This psalm has been called "the mountain psalm" because the King James Version made the first verse read as if it were an affirmation: "I will lift up mine eyes unto the hills, from whence cometh my strength." Since it carried the thought that the psalmist's help came from the hills, countless lovers of the Lord have fallen into the error of ascribing to the mountains the help which actually comes from the mountains' Maker.

The American Revised Version has corrected the mistake

(punctuation errors are human) of a comma and a period in the King James Version. The writer of this psalm was at a distance from the Temple, as will be noted in the psalm which precedes it. Read Psalm 120 carefully, and then Psalm 123. In Psalm 121 the singer lifted up his eyes to the mountain upon which the Temple was built. Then he asked a question and received an immediate answer. The American Revised Version correctly puts it:

> I will lift up mine eyes unto the mountains:
> From whence shall my help come?
> My help cometh from Jehovah,
> Who made heaven and earth.

It is not from the distant and loved mountains, with all their hallowed associated memories, but from Jehovah, that help will come. The psalmist was not a pantheist; for him the marvels of nature, the glories of the heavens, the soughing of the winds among the treetops, were but evidence that God was in all and above all. It cannot be said of the psalmist as has been so truly said of one of our great American naturalists: "He always saw the garden, but he never saw the Gardener."

The psalmist went on to interpret his confidence in his Helper: God will not suffer his foot to be moved; God will keep and protect; God will guide now and forever, no matter where he may be. This man was not singing a Miserere; he was lifting his voice in a shouted Magnificat. The psalm is not a monody in minor; it is an outburst of exuberance.

There is an ascending note in this song; indeed, it is the second of fifteen psalms, beginning with Psalm 120 and concluding with Psalm 134, which are given the ancient heading "A Song of Ascents." One explanation of this heading is that there were fifteen steps in the Temple leading up to the court of Israel and that these fifteen songs were connected with the fifteen steps, being sung on certain ceremonial occasions when the worshipers went up by these steps.

There is another explanation: that these psalms were used on the ascending march of the pilgrims returning from exile in Babylon. As they climbed toward the mountain where the Temple had been set, they solaced their way with these psalms of hope, joy, and triumphant faith.

Regardless of which explanation may be correct, the student of the psalms will readily recognize the ascension of spirit in the one before us. Its entire outlook is up, Godward and therefore victorious. There is a recognition of complete need and a complete assurance of help to supply that need.

Ruskin, in his *Modern Painters,* has called attention to the fact that the greatest painters of Mary and the Son have always a hint of the mountains in the distance, symbols of that mystery of the heights which call to the depths of a man's soul and lift him to the highest ground. "We look not at the things which are seen," but to Him who is seen by faith and in whom we have tranquillity.

Life has its varied appointments, its shadows and its sunshine. But the message of this psalm gives its glad insistence to the fact that above all is God, keeping watch over his own. The psalm is an expression of the unlimited provision of Jehovah for those who look to him, and of his ceaseless watchfulness. God will keep you steady in the midst of unsteadiness; and when you sleep, he will stay awake. He will have you in security, and neither heat nor cold will find you by him unattended. As you go to work and as you return, he will be your protector. And, greatest of all, he will keep your soul.

John McNeil told us once at Northfield about a man who, when he was dying, asked that they should inscribe upon his tombstone just one word, and that one word was not his name nor anything about his life; but over the anonymous corpse that lay beneath was to be the word "Kept." Said the great Scottish preacher: "It was a stroke of genius. Kept! That will do. If I live until I am ninety and do well all that time, when I come to die, put me down in my grave and only put that over the top of me, and I will be full content. Kept!"

From Jehovah cometh our help!

William McKinley

President

March 4, 1897—September 14, 1901

2 Chronicles 1:10

*Give me now wisdom and knowledge, that I may go out **and**
come in before this people; for who can judge this thy people,
that is so great?*

William McKinley

WILLIAM MCKINLEY

Born January 29, 1843, Niles, Ohio.
Died September 14, 1901, Buffalo, New York.

The ancestors of our twenty-fifth President were Scotch-Irish who emigrated to York County, Pennsylvania, in 1743. His great-grandfather served as a private in the War of Independence.

William McKinley was the seventh of nine children. He attended Allegheny College, Meadsville, Pennsylvania, but illness forced him to withdraw before graduation. For a time he taught school, a country school, where doubtless he learned as much as did his pupils.

He was the last of our Presidents who served in the War Between the States; time had all but run out on the "bloody shirt" sure-fire formula for winning high political office. He enlisted as a private in the Twenty-third Ohio Volunteer Infantry; served with exceptional gallantry at Antietam and in the Valley campaigns, especially at Cedar Creek; was promoted to the rank of major on March 14, 1865, and served on the staff of General Rutherford B. Hayes. He was mustered out, with his regiment, on July 26, 1865.

He was nominated for the presidency in June, 1896, at the Republican Convention in St. Louis. His opponent on the Democratic ticket was the gifted orator William Jennings Bryan, who was to run unsuccessfully for the presidency three times (twice against McKinley) and whose nearest approach to that high office was to become secretary of state under Woodrow Wilson.

McKinley was inaugurated President on March 4, 1897, and was re-elected in 1900.

On September 6, 1901, when he was officially welcoming guests at the Pan-American Exposition in Buffalo, New York, he was shot by an anarchist assassin, Leon Czolgosz. He died nine days later.

President McKinley was a kindly and gentle man, singularly pure in his political life, refuting by his conduct the charges so frequently made that he was a political creature of Mark Hanna. The love he gave his invalid wife and the tender care he extended her compose one of the beautiful pages in history.

McKinley was a member of the Methodist Church.

Requisite for Leadership

In that night did God appear unto Solomon, and said unto him, Ask what I shall give thee. And Solomon said unto God, Thou hast showed great loving kindness unto David my father, and hast made me king in his stead. Now, O Jehovah God, let thy promise unto David my father be established; for thou hast made me king over a people like the dust of the earth in multitude. Give me now wisdom and knowledge, that I may go out and come in before this people; for who can judge this thy people, that is so great? And God said to Solomon, Because this was in thy heart, and thou hast not asked riches, wealth, or honor, nor the life of them that hate thee, neither yet hast asked long life, but hast asked wisdom and knowledge for thyself, that thou mayest judge my people, over whom I have made thee king: wisdom and knowledge is granted unto thee; and I will give thee riches, and wealth, and honor, such as none of the kings have had that have been before thee; neither shall there any after thee have the like.

Here are the vision and the prayer of Solomon and the reply from Jehovah, as found in 2 Chronicles 1:7-12. In this passage is the verse chosen by President McKinley for his inauguration on March 4, 1897. (For his second inauguration he chose a passage kindred in theme, Proverbs 16:21-22.)

If ever a man assuming the leadership of a nation had need of wisdom and knowledge, that man was William McKinley. Farm problems; the loud clamor concerning the "free and unlimited coinage of silver"; the aftermath of economic paralysis; the growing conflict between the capitalist dinosaurs and the little men; the ruthless maneuvers to gain control of the sugar cane plantations of Cuba, Puerto Rico, and the Philippines, which were to result in an unnecessary war—all these lay before him as he took the oath of office and raised to his lips the words of Solomon's prayer.

Solomon was the greatest, the wisest, and, in many ways, the most disreputable of the Hebrew kings. He began with such bright prospects, achieved such high honor, led his people to such great prosperity; and then his life ended in such dark shadows that whether he was granted a place among the saved is a matter of continued disagreement.

In Pietro Lorenzetti's great fresco of the resurrection in the Campo Santo at Pisa, Solomon appears in the middle of the picture, looking doubtfully around, not knowing whether he is to be called to the right hand or to the left. As has been said of another, "in him genius was wedded to sin, and success was the author of failure."

Not twenty years old when he was seated on the throne of his father, he became king over a realm resplendent and powerful. Splendidly endowed for the position of king, prepared and trained by his mother Bathsheba, loved with passionate affection by David his father, he had what seemed an assured future. But he had never been taught how to escape from his greatest enemy, himself. Because of this, the fruit of his old age was bitter to his taste, and his dying song was "Vanity of vanities, all is vanity."

Why the contrast between his beginning and his end? The answer is that while God approved of Solomon's choice, he did not approve of Solomon. What is true of all of us was true of Solomon, but in more marked degree because of his greater responsibility: he knew so much better than he produced.

> How much better is it to get wisdom than gold!
> Yea, to get understanding is rather to be chosen than silver.

So wrote Solomon, and when he came to give summation he acknowledged that

> The lot is cast into the lap;
> But the whole disposing thereof is of Jehovah.

Solomon ought to have lived as he taught, you say? So should we all.

Did ever better advice come from man than these inspired instructions which Solomon gave his son?

> Trust in Jehovah with all thy heart,
> And lean not upon thine own understanding:
> In all thy ways acknowledge him,
> And he will direct thy paths.
> Be not wise in thine own eyes;
> Fear Jehovah, and depart from evil.

But his knowledge and performance were not alike.

True knowledge is not mere intellectual affirmation; it is a personal apprehension. One may know, after a fashion, that there is a God; but really to know God implies and demands trust and obedience.

After many years of selfless service, Paul was eager for more of the light which once had blinded him but which he now knew to be the only source of perfect vision. "That I may know him, and the power of his resurrection, and the fellowship of his sufferings, being conformed unto his death," he prayed.

Writing to the church in Corinth, where the inhabitants were as alert and intelligent as the people he addressed on Mars' Hill, Paul warned against a knowledge that "puffeth up." When we become proud of what we know, we are "puffed up," unable to see either our feet or the path on which we walk.

Knowledge *is* power, but only as it is applied. If it is applied for good, it uplifts the world; if it is applied for evil, it destroys the world. The atomic discoveries are an example of what is here meant.

The king, or the President, who has knowledge but lacks love is a danger to the world. Brilliancy of mind must not be placed above goodness; intellectual dexterity must not displace love. How much Byron knew, how sweetly did he sing, but how mean was his life! Of Lord Bacon, it was said:

> How noble his aphorisms, how petty his avarice and envy! What scholarship was his, and what cunning also! With what splendor of argument could he plead for the advancement of learning and liberty, and with what meanness did he take bribes from the rich against the poor. His mind seems like a palace of marble with splendid galleries and library and banqueting hall, yet in this palace the spider spins its web and vermin make the foundations to be a noisome place.

What Jehovah willed for Solomon to have was not knowledge and wisdom apart from any relation to him or sense of dependence upon him. God's estimate of that sort of knowledge and wisdom you find in Isaiah 29:14: "The wisdom of their wise men shall perish, and the understanding of their prudent men shall be hid."

Such wisdom as that referred to in President McKinley's inaugural verses is described by James: "The wisdom that is from above is first pure, then peaceable, gentle, easy to be entreated, full of mercy and good fruits, without variance, without hypocrisy."

Quite evidently, such knowledge is not inherent; it is imparted by God. And quite as evidently, Solomon never attained to it.

Theodore Roosevelt

President

September 14, 1901—March 4, 1909

James 1:22-23

But be ye doers of the word, and not hearers only, deluding your own selves. For if any one is a hearer of the word and not a doer, he is like unto a man beholding his natural face in a mirror.

Theodore Roosevelt

THEODORE ROOSEVELT

Born October 27, 1858, New York City, New York.
Died January 6, 1919, Oyster Bay, New York.

Our twenty-sixth President, like John Tyler, Millard Fillmore, Andrew Johnson, Chester A. Arthur, Calvin Coolidge, Harry S Truman, and Lyndon Baines Johnson, succeeded to the presidency upon the death of his chief.

Although as a boy he was of a naturally frail physique, his strict determination to espouse the out-of-doors life brought ample returns in the strength and vitality upon which he drew so heavily in after years in his pursuit of "the strenuous life."

He graduated from Harvard in the class of 1880; studied law but abandoned it, without qualifying for the bar, in order to enter active politics; and was elected to the New York legislature.

During the presidency of Benjamin Harrison, he was appointed a member of the United States Civil Service Commission, from which he resigned in 1895 to become president of the Board of Police Commissioners of New York City. He became, two years later, assistant secretary of the navy by appointment of President McKinley. This position he resigned to enter the Spanish-American War (which he did much to bring about) with his famous Rough Riders. When his regiment was mustered out, he was nominated for, and elected, governor of New York.

Elected as vice-president on the ticket with McKinley, he became President upon the assassination of McKinley, served out the remainder of the term, and was then elected for a full term.

He ran again for President on the Progressive, or Bull Moose, ticket and was defeated.

President Roosevelt had a wide and incisive comprehension of public affairs; he was a man of decisive action, and one of unquestionable honor. He was a member of the Dutch Reformed Church.

A Doer of the Word

When, on March 4, 1905, Theodore Roosevelt was inaugurated for his first and only elective term as President, he chose for his Scripture text James 1:22-23: "But be ye doers of the word, and not hearers only, deluding your own selves. For if any one is a hearer of the word and not a doer, he is like unto a man beholding his natural face in a mirror."

This remarkable man was nothing if not a doer; he reveled in action, and he gloried in what he so often called "the strenuous life." If Emerson, the great American transcendentalist, was right when he said, "We only really believe what we do," then Theodore Roosevelt qualifies as a believer in getting things done.

James sternly denounced the mere intellectual acknowledgment of Christian truth, as against the practical application of Christian truth to daily conduct. It is, he said in effect, entirely possible to define faith without applying it. "Why," he said, "you are very orthodox; so is the devil," and then proceeded to show wherein. James, the president of the council of Jerusalem, was an intensely practical man who meant business and who would have us heed his friend Paul's admonition "to redeem the time, because the days are evil."

There is in James's letter much resemblance to those sayings of Jesus which we call the Sermon on the Mount; indeed, the epistle of James has more references to these sayings of our Lord than do all the other New Testament letters. Perhaps this is not so strange, since James, being the brother of Jesus, must have looked back and recalled the things which he had heard direct from Jesus or which had been told him.

Another thing to keep in mind in the reading of this letter is that there is no contradiction between it and the epistles of Paul, which emphasize faith even to the point of declaring that not by works, lest any man should boast, but by faith alone in Christ, is a man saved. James is emphatic: a faith which is not expressed in action is simply no faith at all. To quote G. Campbell Morgan:

> If in these words [James 1:22] he urges us to be doers of the Word, we must remember that the Word he refers to is that which he has just described as "the inborn word." He was referring, not merely to any written Word, nor to his Lord as the Word incarnate alone; but to the Word of God received into the soul through the written Word, and by the Word incarnate. That Word is only of real value as it is obeyed, as what it enjoins is done. There is no profit, but rather the reverse, in hearing, if there be no doing.

Actions speak louder than words. How appealing these words of James must have been to our twenty-sixth President, of whom it was said that he wasted no time in "getting on with the business." Indeed, so intent was he in getting on with the business that he frequently left the rights of others trampled in the mud behind him. Witness his grab of the Panama Canal Zone, and his purported remark when by-passing Congressional action: *"Raus mit* the law. I want the Canal built." So, a revolution in Panama, a province seceded from Colombia, the Republic of Panama recognized "tonight and not tomorrow," and the zone leased in perpetuity—all of which was action, though not Christian action.

It is quite possible for a man to go round and round ever so fast but get nowhere. James would be the first to say that a man may sometimes travel faster on his knees than on his feet. But he was mortally tired of those who would say, "Lord, Lord," but do not the things that the Lord commands.

One of Aesop's fables, "The Lark and Her Young Ones," is an apposite illustration of the Scripture verse before us.

There was a brood of young larks in a field of corn just ripe, and the mother looking each day for the reapers, left word that whenever she went out in search of food, her young ones should report to her all the news they heard. One day, while she was absent, the farmer came to look at the state of the crop. "It is full time," said he, "to call in my neighbors and get my corn reaped." When the old lark came home, the young ones told their mother what they had heard and begged her to remove them forthwith. "Time enough," said she; "if he trusts to his neighbors, he will have to wait awhile for his harvest." Next day, however, the owner came again, and finding the sun still hotter, the corn more ripe and nothing done, "There is not a moment to be lost," said he. "We cannot depend upon our neighbors, we must call in our relations." And turning to his son, "Go, call your uncles and cousins and see that they begin tomorrow."

In still greater fear, the young larks repeated to their mother the farmer's words. "If that is all," said she, "do not be frightened, for the relatives have harvest work of their own; but take particular notice what you hear the next time and be sure you let me know."

The owner came the next day, and finding the grain falling to the ground from over-ripeness, called to his son, "We must wait for our neighbors and friends no longer; we will set to work ourselves, tomorrow." When the young larks told their mother this, she said, "Then it is time to be off, indeed; for when a man takes up his business himself instead of talking about it, you may be sure he means business."

It is not what we say that gets things done, but what we do. As James said, the proof of a man's belief in Christ is his manifestation of the Christlike life. To quote another trenchant saying of Emerson's, "how can I hear what you are saying, when what you are keeps ringing in my ears?"

There is an urgency about the epistle of James that has surely escaped us. For who can fail to acknowledge the appalling discrepancy between what we Christians profess to believe and what we do? Does not the failure to accept the personal implications of James 1:22-23 bring to our hearts rebuke beyond expression? Does not the terrible lag in the response of our churches to the Great

Commission betray brutally our sin of inaction, which is born of our unconcern? God help us! It is not what we say, it is what we do, that counts where he keeps books.

William H. Taft

President

March 4, 1909—March 4, 1913

1 Kings 3:9-12

Give thy servant therefore an understanding heart to judge thy people, that I may discern between good and evil; for who is able to judge this thy great people?

And the speech pleased the Lord, that Solomon had asked this thing. And God said unto him, Because thou hast asked this thing, and hast not asked for thyself long life, neither hast asked riches for thyself, nor hast asked the life of thine enemies, but hast asked for thyself understanding to discern justice; behold, I have done according to thy word: lo, I have given thee a wise and an understanding heart; so that there hath been none like thee before thee, neither after thee shall any arise like unto thee.

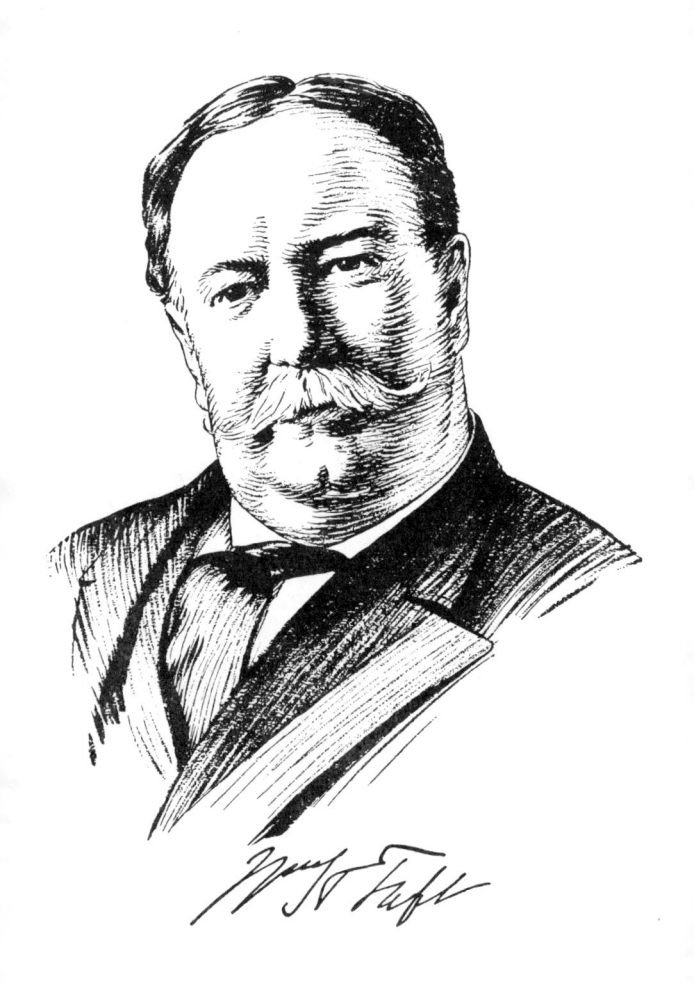

William Howard Taft

Born September 15, 1857, Cincinnati, Ohio.
Died March 8, 1930, Washington, D. C.

The father of William Howard Taft served as both attorney-general and secretary of war in Grant's cabinet, and was also, at other times, a minister to Austria-Hungary and to Russia. Our twenty-seventh President, therefore, had an unusual background of service in the nation's weal and in international affairs.

Taft graduated from high school in Cincinnati. He graduated from Yale in 1878 and, after studying law in Cincinnati College, was admitted to the Ohio bar in 1880. He was elected judge of the Superior Court of Ohio in 1888, and in 1890 was appointed solicitor general of the United States by President Benjamin Harrison. In 1892 he was appointed a judge of the Sixth Circuit Court. For four years, 1901-1904, he served as president of the Philippine Commission and governor ex officio of the Philippines. In 1904 he returned to the United States to become secretary of war. In June, 1908, he was nominated for President by the Republican party in Chicago, and in November was elected over William Jennings Bryan.

In the factional dispute within the Republican party, in which the liberal wing was led by Theodore Roosevelt and the conservative wing by Taft, Taft's middle-of-the-road attitude was an amiable object of attack, and as a result he was overwhelmingly defeated when he ran for a second term. His was not a nature to carry grudges, and he found in the Supreme Court a wide avenue for his distinct judicial gifts. Here he served as chief justice for nine years, after which he retired because of ill health, just a month before his death.

President Taft was a Unitarian in church relationship.

A Prayer for Discernment

If you visit the Mission Inn at Riverside, California, you will be shown the chair in which President Taft sat while a guest there. It is a large chair—Mr. Taft was a very large man. Also, it does not look to be a very comfortable chair. And the presidential chair was never one of comfort for William Howard Taft, our twenty-seventh President.

The Scripture text he chose for his inauguration on March 4, 1909, was 1 Kings 3:9-12, which contains Solomon's prayer for wisdom to judge the people.

God, full of gracious kindness, gave Solomon more than he asked, and in fact, added those things for which he doubtless had wished but which he had wisely refrained from bringing before Jehovah in his petition. What had gone before—how he had made his decision and what had entered into the making of it—we are not told. By what means, and through what labyrinthine turnings, Solomon came to his choice, we cannot know; but the grandeur and the wisdom of that choice are unassailable. What he prayed for was discernment and understanding in the administering of his duty.

Prayer, for some, is only for emergencies. Danger appears, sickness comes, bread is lacking, a job is lost, difficulties arise—then they pray. An infidel down in the coal mine, when the shoring gave way, began to pray. Said a Christian fellow miner, listening to him, "Sure, and there's naught like a slab of coal to make a man pray."

But prayer is more than asking for things. Prayer is helplessness casting itself on power; prayer is ignorance seeking wisdom; prayer is feebleness courting strength.

What hinders us in prayer? Tagore, that Indian poet-mystic, has laid his finger on the secret:

> I came out alone on my way to my tryst. But who is this that follows me in the silent dark?
>
> I move aside to avoid his presence but I escape him not.
>
> He makes the dust rise from the earth with his swagger; he adds his loud voice to every word that I utter.
>
> He is my own little self, my lord, he knows no shame; but I am ashamed to come to thy door in his company.

We must remember, in discussing the problems of prayer, that we ourselves are the number one problem. This was in the mind of David when he said, in Psalm 66:18, "If I regard iniquity in my heart, the Lord will not hear." Isaiah put it thus: "Your iniquities have separated between you and your God, and your sins have hid his face from you" (Isaiah 59:2).

If Solomon was correct in laying aside the good, but lesser, issues and asking for the greatest (and God evidently judged him to have done that thing), is it not true that we should stand on the same high ground? We, too, must make a choice, and all the issues of our lives hinge upon our choice. Moreover, we cannot know what to choose unless we petition him who alone has complete knowledge. We cannot pray until first we have prayed! It is only through prayer that we can have clearness of conception as to what are the fundamental choices.

Nowhere in our modern church life have we so far departed from the New Testament pattern as in this matter of prayer. Take just one verse (be not bothered by those who sneer at "proof texts"!): "And they continued steadfastly in the apostles' teaching and fellowship, in the breaking of bread and the prayers" (Acts 2:42). No wonder the early Christians turned the world upside down, which means that they turned it right side up. They believed in prayer. It never occurred to them to consider prayer as a sort of vocal exercise. They believed that through prayer things would be brought about that would not be brought about if they did not pray.

We are never so high as when we are on our knees. When we pray, God works.

God holds out to us today, as he did to Solomon at Gibeon, the scepter of his power. He longs to supply our needs according to the riches of his glory, to strengthen us with power through the Holy Spirit in the inner man, to give us an understanding heart so that we can discern between good and evil and, discerning it, make that choice which pleases him.

God wants us to pray. Of that we may be certain. Luke 11:1 is often quoted with an added word which entirely changes its meaning. One of the disciples—which one we are not told—who had been present on one of the occasions when the Lord had met with God in prayer and who had felt the ineffable sublimity of that experience had made the eager entreaty: "Lord, teach us to pray." Not "teach us *how* to pray," as it is so frequently misquoted, but "teach us *to* pray." We know *how;* we *do* not. James declared, "Ye have not, because ye ask not." Either we do not ask; or if we do ask, we ask amiss, because what we want, we want for ourselves.

Prayer is the lifting up of the living soul to the living God. David said, in Psalm 25:1, "Unto thee, O Jehovah, do I lift my soul." Archbishop Trench declared, "We must not conceive of prayer as overcoming God's reluctance, but as laying hold of His highest willingness."

What is prayer? Some twenty-five years ago, a friend gave me a little paper-bound book, printed in London, written by "An Unknown Christian," and entitled *The Kneeling Christian*. It has meant much to me and to hundreds to whom its truth has gone. Here is the unknown author's answer to "What is prayer?"

It is a sign of the spiritual life. I should as soon expect life in a dead man as spiritual life in a prayerless soul. Our spirituality and our fruitfulness are always in proportion to the reality of our prayers. If, then, we have at all wandered away from home in the matter of prayer, let us today resolve, "I will arise and go unto my Father, and say unto Him, 'Father'." At this point, I laid down my pen, and on the page of the first paper I picked up were these words: "The secret of failure is that we see men, rather than God. Romanism trembled, when Luther saw God. Scotland fell prostrate, when John Knox saw God. The world became the parish of one man, when Wesley saw God. Multitudes were saved, when Whitefield saw God. Thousands of orphans were fed, when George Muller saw God. All London went over the river to hear Charley, when Spurgeon saw God. And He is the same yesterday, today and forever."

Woodrow Wilson

President

March 4, 1913—March 4, 1921

Psalm 119:43-46

And take not the word of truth utterly out of my mouth;
For I have hoped in thine ordinances.
So shall I observe thy law continually
For ever and ever.
And I shall walk at liberty;
For I have sought thy precepts.
I will also speak of thy testimonies before kings,
And shall not be put to shame.

Woodrow Wilson

Woodrow Wilson

Born December 28, 1856, Staunton, Virginia.
Died February 3, 1924, Washington, D. C.

Every visitor to Staunton, that lovely old Virginia city situated at the head of the Shenandoah Valley, is reminded that our twenty-eighth President was born in the manse of the Staunton Presbyterian Church, of which his father was pastor. He was named Thomas Woodrow, after his maternal grandfather Thomas Woodrow, but rarely did President Wilson use both his given names.

Woodrow Wilson entered Princeton in 1875 and graduated four years later. He studied law at the University of Virginia, but gave up law to study government and history. He received his Ph.D. from Johns Hopkins University in 1886. After teaching for four years at Bryn Mawr, he became, in 1890, a member of the faculty at Princeton. In 1902 he entered upon his distinguished career as president of Princeton, and in 1910 he was elected governor of New Jersey on the Democratic ticket.

In an exciting contest with the popular Champ Clark of Missouri, he was nominated for the presidency by the Democratic Convention which met in Baltimore in 1912, the intriguing figure of William Jennings Bryan making Wilson's nomination possible. The split in the Republican ranks that resulted from the course pursued by Theodore Roosevelt elected Wilson for his first term. Four years later he was re-elected only because Hiram Johnson's hatred of Charles Evans Hughes enabled him to carry California.

Woodrow Wilson was a character of noble aspirations and the

embodiment of keen and compelling logic. He was a member of the Presbyterian Church.

Unashamed Before Kings

On his second inauguration day, March 4, 1917, Woodrow Wilson touched his lips to Psalm 119, verses 43-46.

What a prophetic selection that was, and what a marked description of the truly great man who was to face the remaining kings of the world in the Hall of Mirrors at Versailles to sign, on June 28, 1919, the treaty of peace with Germany, which treaty was rejected by the United States Senate on March 19, 1920. So far as Woodrow Wilson was concerned, though his dream of the United States leading out in a League of Nations did not come into actuality, he himself was not "put to shame."

Not until the presidency of Franklin D. Roosevelt were there as momentous decisions to be made as those which came to Woodrow Wilson, full-freighted with destiny. On January 31, 1917, a month before Wilson's second inauguration, Germany announced unrestricted submarine warfare; three days later diplomatic relations were severed; and on April 2, before a special session of Congress, President Wilson asked for a declaration of war. Surely he had need of utter dependence on that text which he had chosen from Psalm 119 for the solemn ceremony of March 4.

The theme of Psalm 119 is the power of the Word of God, his will made known to men. The opening line gives the keynote: the integrity and security of the man who walks in the way of Jehovah and meditates on his statutes. Ours should be the psalmist's plea:

> Open thou mine eyes, that I may behold
> Wondrous things out of thy law.

This world of affairs in which we live is not a friend of truth. President Wilson discovered this in those sordid and cynical days of diplomatic double-talk. There came a day when he realized how utterly without conscience were the leaders of nations when their own interests were involved, and how the weasel words of secret treaties could suck the lifeblood from the brave and heroic sentiments to which, in the open, those leaders penned their signatures.

Well might Wilson have echoed Pilate's sneer: "What is truth?" Though he was no match for those skilled European diplomats, and though his dream crumbled upon his head, the truth by which he tried to steer his course still merits him the esteem of all mankind. It is only when a man observes the law of truth that he can walk in liberty.

What is truth? Let it be ours to search for it, and not ours to sneer at it.

No longer is it true that a man's word is his bond. The simple and basic honesty which gave light in days of darkness has largely deserted the leadership of our nation, as well as those whom they are presumed to lead, so that political machines are never overthrown except by a machine that is stronger and more venal. Investigations which reveal chicanery in high office are shrugged off, or bought off, or simply ignored. Thus the word "politician," which once meant one skilled in political science or administration and was synonymous with "statesman," has now degenerated into a word meaning a spoilsman, or a schemer for private advantage.

More and more we have taken the attitude of Pilate, with his scornful question and his agnostic indifference. God has become but an idea, not a constructive power and controlling concern. The absurdity of presuming that moral standards can be maintained when that from which they draw their inspiration has been discarded ought to be apparent to anyone.

But we refuse to learn; our minds are like concrete, all mixed up and permanently set. Cicero complained of Homer "that he taught the gods to live like men." We still trust in ourselves and in our skill. We are unlike the psalmist, who declared:

> And I shall walk at liberty;
> For I have sought thy precepts.
> I will also speak of thy testimonies before kings,
> And shall not be put to shame.

The opening sentence of Isaiah 32 declares that "a king shall reign in righteousness, and princes shall rule in justice." Then, following a wonderful description of how a righteous man is regarded and of his place in this stormy world, we are told that "the work of righteousness shall be peace, and the effect of righteousness, quietness and confidence forever." Such statements need to be kept before us. The ultimate result of righteousness is peace, and from righteousness only can come quietness and confidence. Peace is impossible so long as righteousness is ignored; that is true in the realm of international relationships, and it is true in the relationship between man and God.

If you say that any procedure other than that which man has pursued through the long centuries is but the vision of impracticability, then ask yourself, "Where has the so-called practical been of any lasting benefit to us?" Belief in God and action thereon is a venture, to be sure. But the venture is, and always has been, justified. When we tie up to the promises of God, we tie up to his unchangeable security and fulfilment. The problems of human relationships are varied and complex. In spite of all the treaties, parliaments, councils, assemblies, courts, and un-united nations, it appears that we move in a vicious circle, because there is lacking the dynamic power to make the dreams of men come true. Christ alone can supply that power.

Come, listen to Peter preaching on the day of Pentecost. Is his subject the problems of race, of intolerance, of distribution of property, of the relation between capital and labor, of the "humanizing" of industry? So far as I can see in the account of that sermon, he said nothing about those things. But he preached that day about a Man who was crucified, who was buried, who rose from the dead, and is now glorified—the Saviour from sin, sitting on the right hand of God.

As men listened, they saw that Christ, they were caught by the passion of his self-emptying and by his compassionate concern for them, they were gripped by his purpose. Because of the compulsion of their love for him they became lovers of others; and "they sold their possessions and goods, and parted them to all, according as any man had need." That is what comes from having "the mind of Christ"—one has a mind for others.

So long as men disregard the Man whom God has appointed to judge the world in righteousness, there can be no peace, no quietness, no confidence. The ignoring of the Son of God was the fatal weakness of the Treaty of Versailles; and it would have been the fatal defect in Wilson's League of Nations had it been adopted by the United States. It is the fatal deficiency in any treaty yet proposed by men, no matter how well-meaning they otherwise may be. The Golden Age cannot be brought about by leaden men.

Warren G. Harding

President

March 4, 1921—August 2, 1923

Micah 6:8

He hath showed thee, O man, what is good; and what doth Jehovah require of thee, but to do justly and to love kindness, and to walk humbly with thy God?

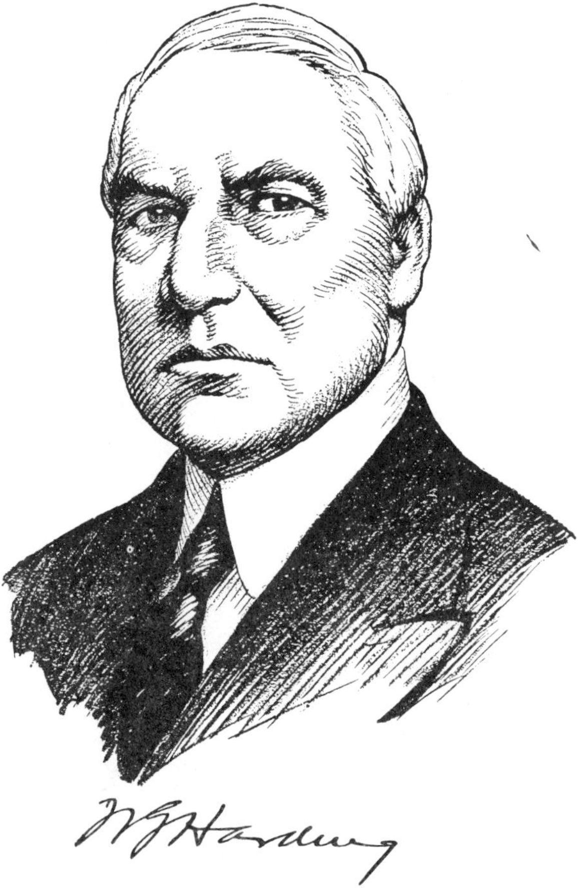
W G Harding

Warren Gamaliel Harding

Born November 2, 1865, Corsica, Ohio.
Died August 2, 1923, San Francisco, California.

The twenty-ninth President of the United States was the son of George T. Harding, a farmer and a country doctor, and Phebe Dickerson Harding. His formal education was limited to attending the public schools and to three years in Ohio Central College. He taught a country school for a year and read law for a short time. In 1884 he became owner and editor of the *Marion Star*, Marion, Ohio.

He served two terms in the Ohio state senate, was lieutenant-governor of the state, and in 1914 was elected to the United States Senate. He opposed the Covenant of the League of Nations, stating that "either the Covenant involves a surrender of national sovereignty and submits our future destiny to the league, or it is an empty thing, big in name, and will ultimately disappoint all of humanity that hinges its hopes upon it."

In the Republican Convention of 1920, he was nominated for President on the tenth ballot. He won the election in a sweeping victory, less because of his own strength than because of the popular reaction against the so-called autocratic actions of President Wilson. He resigned from the Senate in December, 1920, and was inaugurated President on March 4, 1921, becoming the sixth President from Ohio. Three outstanding men were named by him to cabinet positions: Charles E. Hughes, secretary of state; Herbert Hoover, secretary of commerce; and Andrew Mellon, secretary of the treasury. The other members of his cabinet were men of opportunity.

President Harding was a Baptist in his church relationship.

What Jehovah Requires

In the reading room of the beautiful Congressional Library building in Washington, is an alcove dedicated to religion. The committee in charge of selecting a motto for this alcove sent out requests to prominent ministers and religious educators asking for suggestions. The motto finally selected was, "And what doth the Lord require of thee, but to do justly, and to love mercy, and to walk humbly with thy God?" (Micah 6:8 KJV).

It was this verse that President Harding chose for his inauguration on March 4, 1921. Strangely moving words are these. As one goes back in memory to the days of President Harding's brief tenure of office, their tragic futility is the more pronounced in the light of this Scripture selection.

President Harding was likable but weak, one who was in water far beyond his depth. The nation was in a fluid state of mind, with the tide fast ebbing toward an ugly exposure of muddy morals. National weakness was revealed in the simple resolution that officially ended the war between the United States and Germany more than a year after the armistice. After Woodrow Wilson's resounding appeals for the United States to assume the responsibility of world leadership thrust upon it by the war, this resolution was indeed "like hearing the squeak of a timid field mouse after the thunder of battle had rolled away."

The men now living who were soldiers in World War I will, with a disquieting unanimity, tell you that, though they began the war in the spirit of "Lafayette, we are here," they came back with the realization that propaganda was not truth and that it was not quite correct that the war was fought to save democracy. They were fed up, disillusioned, and they had had more than enough of the Old World diplomacy. One of them wrote:

> Amazing is the diplomat—
> He gets us out of trouble
> That we wouldn't get into
> If we had no diplomats.

Thus arose a spirit of cynicism that eventuated in our sense of moral responsibility's literally "going to the dogs."

If only we had made that inaugural verse of President Harding's a part of our national life!

Micah, who wrote this verse, spoke in a time of religious formalism, political unrest, and social decay far worse than anything we have yet known. He represented the princes as feasting upon the poor and taking their fields from them by violence. The prophets were no better; they hated the truth, they loved lies, they were hired hands in the house of God. Justice was abhorred, and equity was perverted. In the palaces of the privileged and in the splendor of the Temple, Micah saw the blood of the exploited and the disinherited.

"They build up Zion," he cried, "with blood, and Jerusalem with iniquity."

The prophet's denunciation reached a climax in the terrible indictment of Micah 3:11, when he accused the magistrates of judging for reward, the priests of teaching for hire, the prophets of divining for money—and covering it all by saying, "Is not Jehovah in the midst of us? No evil shall come upon us!"

I never cease to marvel at the height and depth, the breadth and length of this man Micah, who was a man of the fields. There is no accounting for him, except to say that he was usable in the hands of Jehovah and that he spoke the revealed purpose, plea, and passion of Jehovah.

Verse 8, which Harding chose, is one of the greatest utterances of the Old Testament. In it the prophet takes us a long way toward an understanding of what vital goodness is. Convicted by the divine challenge, the people asked if God would be satisfied with offerings and with the sacrifice of their children. No, said the prophet, God wants, not external ritual, but internal reality. An outward form can never take the place of an inward force. There can be no vital goodness without imparted godliness.

The word "require" used by Micah reveals that such godliness is not optional; it is an imperative. God does not ask it; he commands it. The requirement is a personal requirement, a responsibility of each person. What is commanded of one is commanded of all; none is exempt.

And in saying, "He hath showed thee, O man, what is good," Micah did away with any excuses that might be produced under the guise of ignorance. Note the tense: "He *hath* showed thee." The people were inquiring about a matter concerning which God had already revealed his will. "In religion, too often we are occupied with a quest when we should be launching out on a discovery," someone has well said.

The requirement is, moreover, a minimum requirement. In saying this, I have no thought of giving comfort to those who, in the realm of religion, are minimum-minded, who seek with polite vacuity to discover the least they can "get by with." When I say that the requirement is a minimum one, I mean that it is basic, fundamental, and essential.

"Fear God, and keep his commandments; for this is the whole duty of man," said Solomon. "Thou shalt love the Lord thy God . . . and thy neighbor as thyself," said Jesus.

The charge has frequently been brought against Christians that in them justice, as between man and man, is often looked for in vain. Too frequently we fail to realize the essential relationship

[103]

between creed and conduct, between profession and practice. We ought to remember that the reputation of our Lord is entrusted to us, that we are under inspection constantly.

God does not require, said Micah, that you bring something, that you say something, that you sing something, that you perform something. Not what you bring, but what you are; not your bended knees, your eloquent prayers, your punctilious observances, but your just conduct, your kindly consideration, your humble walk—these are what God requires.

Micah, and Jesus in Matthew 23, how alike! Compare their words, and then let us compare ourselves.

Calvin Coolidge

President

August 2, 1923—March 4, 1929

John 1:23

He said, I am the voice of one crying in the wilderness, Make straight the way of the Lord, as said Isaiah the prophet.

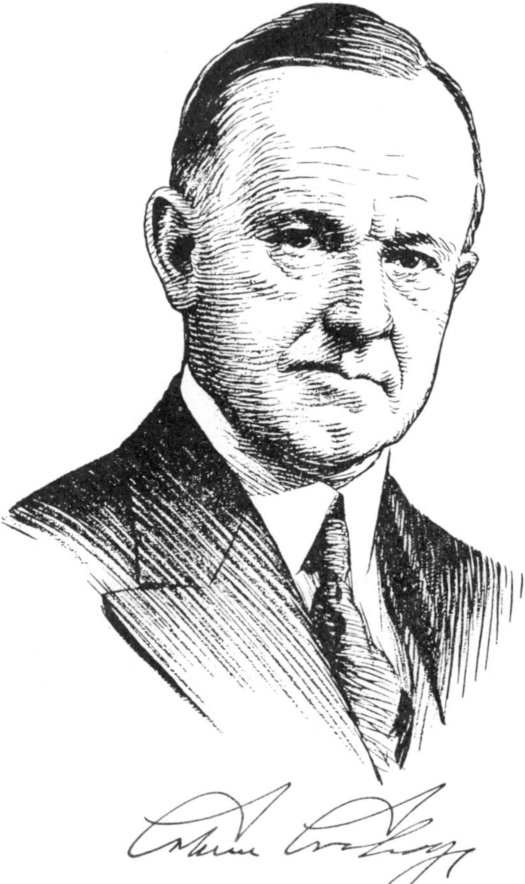

Calvin Coolidge

Born July 4, 1872, Plymouth, Vermont.
Died January 5, 1933, Northampton, Massachusetts.

Calvin Coolidge was born on a farm. His thrifty parents embodied the sturdy virtues of pioneer New England stock. What their farms lacked in rich and fertile soil, the owners made up for by careful and constant tillage.

The future President, upon graduating from Amherst in 1895, studied law in an office in Northampton, Massachusetts, and was admitted to the bar in 1897. He was elected a member of the House of Representatives of Massachusetts in 1907, was a member of the state senate from 1912 to 1915, became lieutenant governor of Massachusetts in 1919. He attracted national attention by the manner in which he handled the policemen's strike in Boston in September of 1919; and in refusing to reinstate the striking men, he incurred the animosity of certain segments of organized labor. This was made an issue in the 1920 campaign for governor, but Coolidge was reelected by a majority of nearly 115,000 out of a total of 510,000 votes. A hint of what was to come nationally was his veto of the bill to increase the pay of members of the Massachusetts House, on the basis that their service was optional and not a means of livelihood; it was a public service and should not be made a job—distinctly not the viewpoint taken of political positions today.

At the Republican Convention of 1920, he was nominated for vice-president by acclamation. Upon the death of Harding, the oath of office of President was administered to Coolidge by his father on August 2, 1923, in the old home of his birth at Plymouth.

Following his second term, having said he did not "choose to run" for President in 1928, he retired to a quiet but active business life in Northampton.

President Coolidge was a member of the Congregational Church.

A Voice in the Wilderness

On a certain spring day in 1927, thousands of people crowded the city of Washington, D. C., and lined Pennsylvania Avenue from the White House grounds to the Capitol building. They had gathered to honor a young man they called "the lone eagle," Charles Lindbergh, and to give him the plaudits he so richly deserved. As the parade made one of those mysterious haltings which come in all parades, the presidential car, in which Lindbergh was riding, stopped directly opposite my box seat (I sat on an orange crate for which I had given a hawker fifty cents), and I found myself looking straight into the face of our thirtieth President.

I gazed at the set lines of President Coolidge's thin face, with that sharp nose and harassed stare, and I imagined he was thinking: "Lindbergh is the man of the hour. Why bother about me, whom am but a President? It is all out of place to dress up this occasion with a President. I've never flown the ocean; I've flown in the face of public opinion, but there is no glamor about that. I wish I could get out and go back to my study. I've work to do."

It was, I say, as if there had been vouchsafed to me a glimpse of the inner mind of this taciturn man, a man who regarded his position as one of imposed trust and of work which things of this sort unpardonably interrupted. It helped me to understand later that laconic statement: "I do not choose to run." He had done his work to the best of his understanding and ability, he had done it faithfully, and now he would have no more of it. Mere politicians could not understand that and sought to twist its meaning. But he just did not have words to waste on men who wasted so many.

In the Scripture passage he chose for his inauguration, "I am the voice of one crying in the wilderness, Make straight the way of the Lord, as said Isaiah the prophet," we have another illustration of how uncannily apt these presidential selections have frequently been.

In John 1:19, the apostle John told of the beginning of that remarkable witness borne to our Lord by John the Baptist. The verse Coolidge selected is John the Baptist's answer to a question from the priests and Levites as to his own identity. "I am the voice of one crying in the wilderness, Make straight the way of the Lord, as said Isaiah the prophet."

What a strange man was this John the Baptist! He was in the wilderness, but he was not a son of the wilderness. Rather, he was a son of the village. His father's name was Zacharias, his mother's Elisabeth. Zacharias was a priest, "of the course of Abijah." If that were all, it would have been nothing, for Josephus tells us that there were more than twenty thousand priests in Judea at this time.

The general character of the priesthood was deeply dyed with the corruption of the age, and our Lord was to describe the priests some thirty years later as blind leaders of the blind. But not so Zacharias, for Luke, who gave us the story of the Baptist's birth, said:

There was in the days of Herod, king of Judea, a certain priest named Zacharias, of the course of Abijah: and he had a wife of the daughters of Aaron, and her name was Elisabeth. And they were both righteous before God, walking in all the commandments and ordinances of the Lord blameless (Luke 1:5-6).

"Righteous before God"! Such were the parents of the man who was to "go before his [God's] face in the spirit and power of

Elijah, to turn the hearts of the fathers to the children, and the disobedient to walk in the wisdom of the just; to make ready for the Lord a people prepared for him."

Well-born, tenderly loved, taught the Scriptures by his priest father, dedicated to the stern life of a Nazirite, separated from a sensual world, subduing his passions and not subdued by them, John went to the desert to learn what was the will of God for him and how to discharge that will. In the desert solitude, he found new meaning in the prophecy of Isaiah and in the character of Elijah, and he came to realize that his greatest strength was in the inner man, where dwelt the spirit.

"There came a man, sent from God, whose name was John." "Sent from God!" That explains why the people left the city to come to the desert to hear him—a preacher clad in a coat of coarse camel's hair, eating locusts and wild honey, living in a cave such as had sheltered David, drinking the water of the little streams. And what did they come forth to hear? They heard the stern gospel of repentance, its deep and revolutionary character typified by burial baptism in the swift waters of the Jordan.

There was nothing soft about the man, or the substance of his message: "Bring forth therefore fruits worthy of repentance." I have often wondered if Zaccheus had not heard that sermon and caught from it the first glimpse of something which impelled him to hear the Christ and then to say, "Behold, Lord, the half of my goods I give to the poor; and if I have wrongfully exacted aught of any man, I restore fourfold."

F. B. Meyer, in his little book *John the Baptist,* has this pertinent paragraph:

There are three signs of a prophet:
  a. Vision
  b. A deep conviction of sin and impended judgment
  c. The gushing forth of moving and eloquent speech

Each of these was apparent in the exalted and extreme degree in John the son of Zacharias.

John the Baptist was not an agitator, a haranguer of crowds, a metaphorical mesmerizer with an ax to grind and an eye for the pinnacle pulpit. He did not invent his message; he had it straight from God, and he gave it straight to the hearts of his listeners.

John's life was not a lengthy one; he lived but long enough to watch his followers turn from him and become disciples of the One whose shoes he declared he was not worthy to unloose. "He must increase, but I must decrease." Read again that tribute paid him by our Lord in Luke 7:24-28. Yes, indeed, he was much more than a prophet. He was a voice crying, "Behold, the Lamb of God, that taketh away the sin of the world!" And those who heard him believed him.

John the Baptist was not born for a king's palace; he was destined for a king's dungeon. But for him the words Paul wrote to the Colossian Christians form a fitting epitaph:

"For ye died, and your life is hid with Christ in God. When Christ, who is our life, shall be manifested, then shall ye also with him be manifested in glory."

Herbert Hoover

President

March 4, 1929—March 4, 1933

Proverbs 29:18

*Where there is no vision, the people cast off restraint;
But he that keepeth the law, happy is he.*

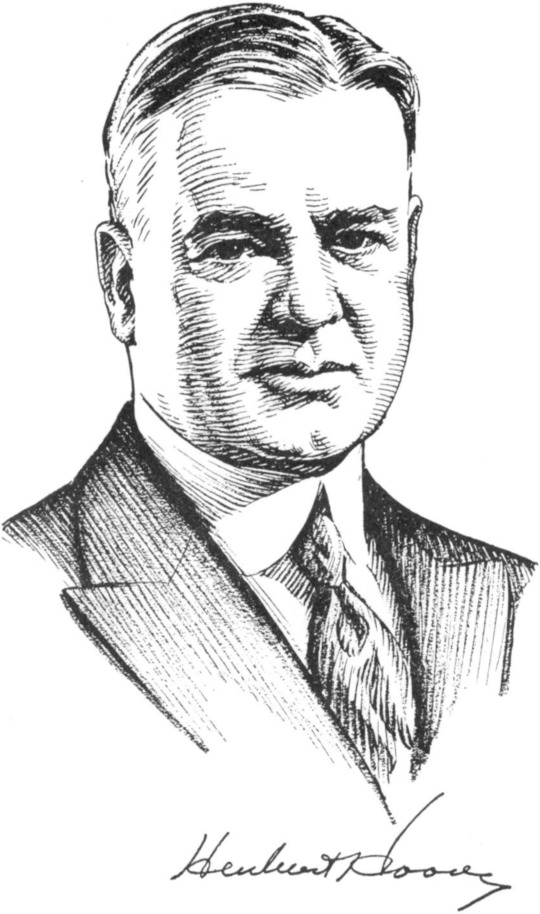
Herbert Hoover

Herbert Clark Hoover

Born August 10, 1874, West Branch, Iowa.
Died October 20, 1964, New York City

One of the few addresses by any citizen of this country which deserves to be called outstanding, and called that without reservation, is that delivered by Herbert Hoover on the occasion of his birthday-homecoming, August 10, 1948, at West Branch, Iowa. It is entitled "The Meaning of America" and should be required reading in every high school, college, and university. In it Hoover referred to the hardships of his early days and to his childhood in his uncle's home (he had been left an orphan when he was nine years old). He spoke tenderly of the public school teacher who meant so much to him; he told of the dependable Quaker stock from which he came; and he reviewed his years of service, national and international. Out of these experiences, he said, he came to understand what our country means.

The address is a moving one and reveals the man in a manner not to be found in the biographical material of *Who's Who in America* under the heading of "Hoover, Herbert, thirty-first President of the United States."

Herbert Hoover, who had served the nation and the world with quiet efficiency in war and in peace, was elected President of the United States in 1928 by an overwhelming majority. It was his first elective office. On March 4, 1929, as he took the oath of office, the economic, political, and social structure of the world was beginning to collapse. Thus he became heir of a catastrophe for which he was not responsible and which, in spite of all his efforts to overcome it, finally brought the country to its most tragic peacetime hour.

Charged with the responsibility for all these ills and smeared with consummate skill by political foes who were in no degree hampered by conscience, he was defeated for a second term.

In religion, he was a Quaker.

The Lost Chord

Sir Arthur Sullivan wrote the music for "The Lost Chord" at midnight as he sat by the deathbed of his brother. In the meditation of that hour, he seemed to feel that what we call life is a chord of music struck on the great organ of being by the hand of the master Musician. And as his brother slipped away into that bourn whence no traveler has ever returned, Sir Arthur's soul poured out its longing and its hope in the music we have come to love so well.

Such intuitive understanding, such imaginative conception, such vision have become almost a lost chord among us. We have grown too sophisticated to permit the harboring of ideals or to be steered by a star.

Consider the Scripture text chosen by Herbert Hoover for his inauguration on March 4, 1929:

> Where there is no vision, the people cast off restraint;
> But he that keepeth the law, happy is he.

And consider the well-nigh universal disregard of that admonition. Vision cannot live, much less flourish, in the soul of the cynic.

President Hoover, an idealist, a man of vision, was compelled to breathe an atmosphere of callous disregard for anything but profit-taking, an atmosphere such as this country had never known before, not even in the days of Jackson's assault on the Bank of America. In James Truslow Adams' astringent words, "Harding had to liquidate the war; Coolidge had to quietly liquidate the scandals of the Harding regime; and Hoover had to watch the liquidation of the Coolidge prosperity."

There has never been a more perfect setting in which to enunciate the truth that "where there is no vision, the people cast off restraint." The Hebrew word which in the King James Version is rendered "perish," has been more carefully translated in the American Revised Version "cast off restraint." The word means literally to break loose. This is the condition of anarchy—a refusal to be bound by law, to abide either by man's pledged word or by God's clear command, referred to as "the law" in Proverbs 29:18.

Vachel Lindsay, in a protest against the spirit of iconoclasm, speaks of "the star-proud fury of men"—vision aroused against pragmatism. Only in "star-proud fury" will men become clear-eyed enough to do away with the indecencies, with the shameful dishonesty and corruption, with the attitudes that the only thing that matters is what we mistakenly call reality.

Out of the shambles of our civilization we are beginning to understand that the man of vision has market value, that, after all, reality and realism are to be had, not in the narrow confines of the seen, but in the limitless spaces of the unseen.

Hitler's lack of vision hurled him and the world into an inferno of welter and ruin. If it be objected that Hitler did have a vision, that he saw a united Germany and a military power superior to that of the Holy Roman Empire, then my reply is that he had no vision whatsoever. He was a visionary, a conjuror of conspiracies, a fanatic possessed by unrestrained ambition, a man like those described by Jude as—

clouds without water, carried along by winds; autumn trees without fruit, twice dead, plucked up by the roots; wild waves of the sea, foaming out their own shame; wandering stars, for whom the blackness of darkness hath been reserved forever.

A man of vision is more than a dreamer. A man of vision, seeing a burning bush unconsumed, turned aside to see what was the portent of this strange thing, and then went into action. Had he been a dreamer, he would have sat down to write a rhapsody about the smoke which got in his eyes.

Paul was a man of vision. While breathing out curses and bent on the death of those called by the name of Christ, he suddenly heard the Voice and was struck blind. From that day he set himself to carry out the commission given him, not by man, but by the very mouth of God. And he justified his long life of hardship by saying to a king, "Wherefore . . . I was not disobedient unto the heavenly vision." His vision had made him a prisoner in a hostile court.

Men who have no vision of what they are doing, no vision of the consequences of their actions, do not envisage society or their obligations to it. A quotation from Herbert Hoover's homecoming address on his seventy-fourth birthday is apposite:

At the time our ancestors were proclaiming that the Creator had endowed all mankind with rights of freedom as the child of God, with a free will, there was being proclaimed by Hegel and later by Karl Marx a satanic philosophy of agnosticism and that the rights of man came from the State. The greatness of America today comes from one philosophy, the despair of Europe from the other.

There are today fuzz-minded people in our country who would compromise in these fundamental concepts. They scoff at these tested qualities in men. They never have understood and never will understand what the word "America" means.

. . . .

It is those moral and spiritual qualities in free men which fulfill the meaning of the word "American." And with them will come centuries of further greatness to our country.

Thus spoke a man of vision. His vision was spiritual, the lost chord in our body politic.

There is a vision for every man, and it may come in the most commonplace circumstances of life. Where could you find a more unlikely spot for Paul to meet Christ and be given that imperative command than on the Damascus road, a burning sun beating down upon his head, the scorching sand beneath his feet? Where could you find a more unlikely abode for a man who would see the world as no man since apostolic times had seen it than that tiny combination of home and cobbler's shop that was Carey's, or a more unlikely man to have such a vision than William Carey?

Men are useful only as they discover for themselves what God's will is for them. Why should we doubt the reality of the heavenly vision for us? Let us thank God for that which can, if we will permit it, impel us to a vaster thing than dust composes.

Franklin D. Roosevelt

President

March 4, 1933—April 12, 1945

1 Corinthians 13

If I speak with the tongues of men and of angels, but have not love, I am become sounding brass, or a clanging cymbal. And if I have the gift of prophecy, and know all mysteries and all knowledge; and if I have all faith, so as to remove mountains, but have not love, I am nothing. And if I bestow all my goods to feed the poor, and if I give my body to be burned, but have not love, it profiteth me nothing. Love suffereth long, and is kind; love envieth not; love vaunteth not itself, is not puffed up, doth not behave itself unseemly, seeketh not its own, is not provoked, taketh not account of evil; rejoiceth not in unrighteousness, but rejoiceth with the truth; beareth all things, believeth all things, hopeth all things, endureth all things. Love never faileth: but whether there be prophecies, they shall be done away; whether there be tongues, they shall cease; whether there be knowledge, it shall be done away. For we know in part, and we prophesy in part; but when that which is perfect is come, that which is in part shall be done away. When I was a child, I spake as a child, I felt as a child, I thought as a child: now that I am become a man, I have put away childish things. For now we see in a mirror, darkly; but then face to face: now I know in part; but then shall I know fully even as also I was fully known. But now abideth faith, hope, love, these three; and the greatest of these is love.

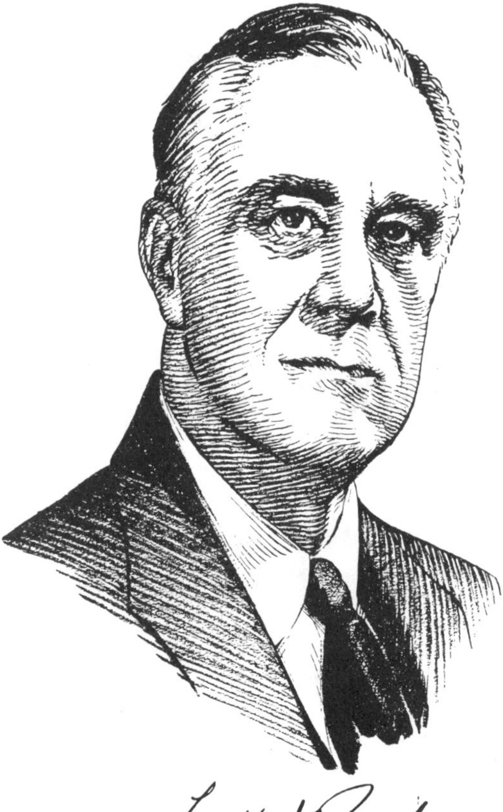

Franklin Delano Roosevelt

Born January 30, 1882, Hyde Park, New York.
Died April 12, 1945, Warm Springs, Georgia.

The thirty-second President of the United States was a fifth cousin of Theodore Roosevelt, the twenty-sixth President. Both were graduates of Harvard. Franklin Delano Roosevelt was born to wealth and social position, but he was also a born politician—without doubt the most skilful and consummate politician who ever occupied the presidential seat. He learned his first statecraft lessons in the atmosphere of New York City, then served in the state legislature and was governor of the state for two terms. Under President Wilson he served as assistant secretary of the navy.

Upon his election as President, he turned the full power of the government's ability to borrow money for all known, and many hitherto untried, avenues of public works. Where millions had been previously spent, he made the country realize that his New Deal would require billions. His radio voice was not equalled before or since; that voice alone quieted the storms of strife and quelled any suspicions as to the ultimate safety of such a gigantic public debt.

He was the leader of this nation through all the perils of World War II; for when he died suddenly at Warm Springs, victory was already an assured fact. The only President ever to be elected for more than two terms (he was elected for four), he will be best remembered in after years for the courageous spirit in which he overcame his physical handicap. Rarely in the history of public life has there been a figure like him. Where men of greater stature hesitated, he met issues head on; and by sheer force of his personality and by his mellifluous radio "fireside chats," he bent both men and issues to his own will.

He was a member of the Episcopal Church.

The Greatest of These

In the thirteenth chapter of 1 Corinthians, used by President Franklin D. Roosevelt for all four of his inaugurations, God reveals to us what is best by setting before us for comparison that which is good. After Paul had gone through the list of great gifts in the experiences of mankind, he closed with the comparison: "But now abideth faith, hope, love, these three; and the greatest of these is love."

To write to first-century Corinthians about love was an exceedingly bold thing. Corinth was the most immoral city in the known world, and to every Corinthian the word "love" was a synonym for immorality. This is the reason for the use of the word "charity" in the King James Version. To avoid the earthly and sensual connotations of *amor,* Jerome had used *caritas,* which had no suggestiveness of this sort, in the Vulgate. When Wycliffe translated from the Vulgate, he transliterated the Latin word *caritas,* and so came the word "charity"; and the King James Version did the same thing. Since the days of King James the word "charity" has greatly changed in meaning; hence, the present-day revisers have returned to the use of the word "love."

Said Harnack of 1 Corinthians 13: "It is the strongest, greatest thing that Paul ever wrote." The whole chapter is a spectrum analysis of love, for like light, the chapter has in it all the colors in combination.

All the things which Paul mentioned as being inferior to love are tremendous—superlative, if you please. The possession of any one of them would have set him or any one of us apart.

"If I speak with the tongues of men and of angels, but have not love, I am become sounding brass, or a clanging cymbal." In less elegant language, it was as if he were saying that without love all speech, be it of men or of angels, is nothing but noise.

"If I have ... all knowledge; and if I have all faith ... but have not love, I am nothing." What could not a man do if he had *all* knowledge and *all* faith? These are high things, things for which men have sought and sought in vain.

"If I bestow all my goods to feed the poor, and if I give my body to be burned, but have not love, it profiteth me nothing." Love is the strength, the dynamic of service; it furnishes the energy and equipment for service.

Certainly, for moral elevation there is nothing in literature equal to this chapter. Note the simple words: "Love suffereth long, and is kind ... envieth not; ... vaunteth not itself, is not puffed up, doth not behave itself unseemly, seeketh not its own, is not provoked."

At this point it is worth while to note the King James translation of that last phrase, "is not easily provoked." The word "easily" is not found in any manuscript. Why was it inserted by the King James translators? Was it because, as Dr. G. Campbell Morgan suggests, the scholars of that day, godly men, remarkable men, felt that Paul was going a little too far, that they slipped in the word? What the inspired statement is declaring is indeed beyond most of us who live in the presence of constant irritants. It simply says that love is not provoked at all!

Then Paul went on to say that love does not keep a ledger. It "takes no account of evil" and finds no satisfaction in any wrongdoing. Rather, it rejoices in the truth.

Such love as Paul wrote about would forever put an end to gossip, slander, and vilification.

> Good name in man and woman, dear my lord,
> Is the immediate jewel of their souls:
> Who steals my purse steals trash; 'tis something, nothing;
> 'Twas mine, 'tis his, and has been slave to thousands;
> But he that filches from me my good name
> Robs me of that which not enriches him
> And leaves me poor indeed.
>
> —SHAKESPEARE

Love, Paul said, "beareth all things"—"beareth" here meaning, not to carry, but to shelter, as with a shield. Love is free from suspicion and looks forward to the day of light in the days of darkness. Love stays true and endures even to the end; it never faileth. Again quoting Shakespeare:

> Love is not love
> Which alters when it alteration finds.

In one of Cyrus Townsend Brady's novels there is a beautiful reference to another verse which illustrates the unchanging quality of love. After a terrible storm at sea, there was washed up on the shore the body of a woman. The sea had torn from her everything which might have served for identification except a plain gold band, a wedding ring. Thinking there might be a name engraved inside it, the people removed the ring, only to find, not a name, but a Scripture reference, 2 Corinthians 12:15. They opened a Bible, and this is what they read: "I will very gladly spend and be spent for you; though the more abundantly I love you, the less I be loved."

Love never faileth! It rings like the sound of a silver bell above the wild cacophony of our rebellious world.

When Paul came to the summation, he sang, "Now abideth faith, hope, love, these three; and the greatest of these is love."

Through faith righteousness pours into the soul, the imputed and imparted righteousness of Jesus Christ, our Savior and our

Lord. "Faith," says F. W. Robertson, "is that strong, buoyant confidence in God and in His love which gives energy and spirit to do right without doubt or despondency."

As faith abides, so does hope. In the gallery of the Vatican the pilgrim reads upon one side the Christian inscriptions copied from the catacombs; and on the other side, inscriptions from the Roman temples. On the Roman side a single sigh echoes along the line of white marble: "Farewell, farewell, and forever, farewell." But on the Christian side are these words: "He who dies in Christ, dies in peace and hope."

Into the pale unknown shall someday slip all upon which a man builds his greatness—his knowledge, his eloquence, his goods, all those things which the world sees and to which it gives applause. The shouting and the tumult all shall die, whether heard in Yalta or in Washington, in convention halls, or on inaugural platforms —shall die as a dream dies at the opening of day. But these things will abide, faith and hope and love. The scaffolding will drop decayed and useless, but these will remain, the temple for which the scaffold was erected.

Harry S Truman

President

April 12, 1945—

Matthew 5:9

Blessed are the peacemakers: for they shall be called the sons of God.

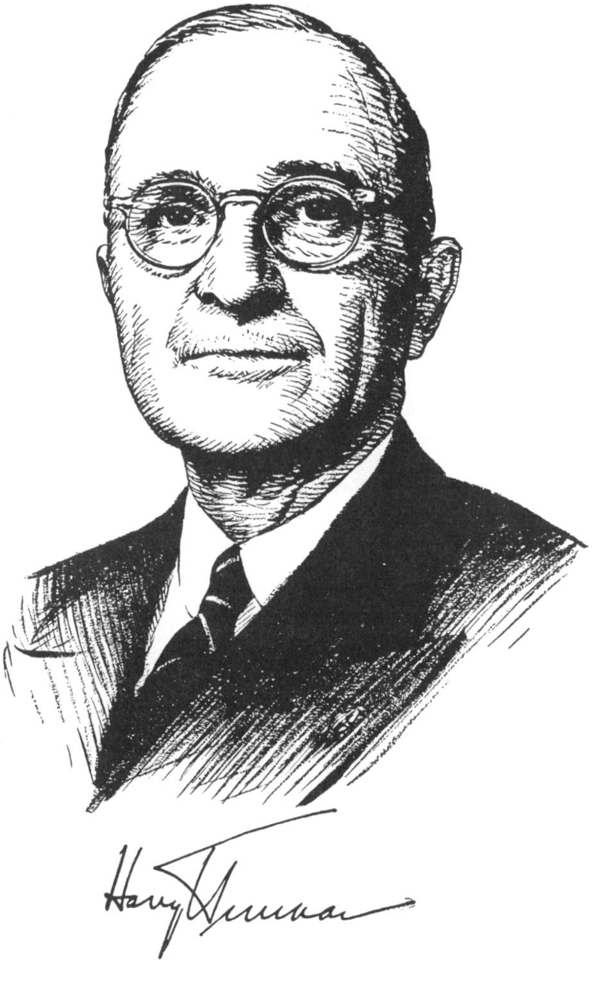

HARRY S TRUMAN

Born May 8, 1884, Lamar, Missouri.
Died December 26, 1972, Kansas City, Missouri.

Harry S Truman, the thirty-third President of the United States, came from the good midwestern stock which has played so formative a role in the life of our nation. He received his education in the public schools of Independence, Missouri, and for a time studied law in the Kansas City School of Law. In 1922 he became judge of the Jackson County Court, a position which did not necessitate admittance to the bar.

During World I, he was in combat service in France as first lieutenant of Battery F, and later as captain of Battery D, 120th Field Artillery, 35th Division. He was discharged with the rank of major.

He was elected to the United States Senate in 1934, re-elected in 1940, and was elected vice-president in 1944. Truman did not seek the vice-presidency, but was selected when it was certain that Wallace as running mate would be a handicap to Roosevelt. Truman "just dropped into the slot. It was agreed that Truman was the man who would hurt him least." When the Trumans walked out of the pandemonium of the convention hall into the Chicago night, accompanied by Secret Service men, Bess Truman asked, "Are we going to have to go through this all the rest of our lives?" He succeeded to the presidency on the death of President Roosevelt on April 12, 1945.

To the astonishment of everyone except Mr. Truman himself, he was re-elected President on November 2, 1948. His training in the rough, tough politics of the Democratic machine of Kansas

City stood him in good stead during the campaign, and he took his plea to the people in one of the most vigorous and amazing speaking tours in the history of the nation.

On the other side, the Republican campaign was conducted with a smug, confident-of-victory attitude. The result was that the man no one wanted in June, everyone wanted in November.

Mr. Truman was a Baptist.

Blessed Be the Peacemakers

Sometimes it comes about that what the great do is the result of what those not great request. A note signed by Robert C. Gooch, chief, General Reference and Bibliography Division, Legislative Reference Service, U. S. Government, November 26, 1948, read thus:

No particular Bible verse was used by President Truman when he took the oath of office on April 12, 1945. An article in the *New York Times* of Friday, April 13th (p. 1, col. 7) reads in part as follows, "Mr. Truman had picked up a Bible from the end of the big Cabinet conference table, held it with his left hand, and placed his right hand upon the upper cover. After repeating the oath, he bowed his head, lifted the Bible to his lips and kissed it."

A few days after receiving this note, I was at the Tulsa airport waiting for a plane to Richmond, when Senator Robert S. Kerr came in from Washington. On sudden impulse, I told him of the incident as related in the *New York Times* and asked him if he would please suggest to Mr. Truman that for his coming inauguration he select a Scripture passage.

Sunday morning, January 16, Senator Kerr called me from Washington and said: "I have attended to that little commission you asked me to handle. The President will use the fifth chapter of Matthew." Thus it was that on March 20, 1949, President Harry S Truman, the thirty-third President of the United States, pressed his lips to that portion of the New Testament which contains the seventh beatitude.

Long ago Milton wrote words so descriptive and so true of our beloved land that we have dared to believe it was to these United States that he referred:

[133]

Methinks I see in my mind a noble and puissant nation rousing herself like a strong man after sleep, and shaking her invincible locks. Methinks I see her as an eagle mewing her mighty youth, and kindling her undazzled eyes at the full mid-day beam.

What is there that concerns this noble and puissant nation today that means more to it than peace? Indeed, is there anything that the whole world desires more than peace? Peace, which would bring freedom from fear of reprisals. Peace, which would lift the burden of multibillion-dollar indebtedness from the backs of men both rich and poor. Peace, which would mean no more agony of searing, flaming death for innocent women and children. Peace, which would see no more the blood drops of anguished mother-hearts for their soldier dead. Peace, which would mean the end of fratricidal death, or destruction and rapine.

When nations sleep with one eye open, gun in hand, waiting for the stealthy dropping of bomb or paralyzing bacteria, when tension, fear, and suspicion are the food on which men feed, there can be no peace. Human attempts to force the dream of peace into actuality have been costly failures, resulting only in more battles, blood, tyranny, oppression, and bitter anguish.

The full scope of scriptural truth is ample basis for saying that the peace referred to in Matthew 5:9 is not a peace which perches on the still smoking, though now for the moment silent, cannon mouth. Christ's constant thought was to harmonize men who have ever gone wrong with the God who is timelessly right. The peace he spoke about, and for which he lived and died, had to be made. It had to be made, and he made it.

The peace of God, being the result of the wisdom and holiness of God, is not to be obtained by either the cleverness or the goodness of men.

Said Jesus: "My peace I give unto you: not as the world giveth."

And then he sent his followers out into a hostile world to be peacemakers in the name of him who is our peace.

For he is our peace, who made both one, and brake down the middle wall of partition, having abolished in his flesh the enmity, even the law of commandments contained in ordinances, that he might create in himself of the two one new man, so making peace; and might reconcile them in one body unto God through the cross, having slain the enmity thereby: and he came and preached peace to you who were far off, and peace to them that were nigh: for through him we both have our access in one Spirit unto the Father (Ephesians 2:14-18).

Peace, for man and for nations, can never be realized apart from God. We cannot defy his will, we cannot flout his Son, we cannot reject his Spirit, and have peace.

> Peace, perfect peace, in this dark world of sin?
> The blood of Jesus whispers peace within.
>
> . . . .
>
> Peace, perfect peace, our future all unknown?
> Jesus we know, and He is on the throne.

President Truman could have urged upon us nothing more pleasing to God than that we dedicate ourselves to peacemaking. The verse he chose is a missionary rallying call, and only by it can the discordances of the world be harmonized. Through Christ alone can racial, social, and personal animosities be resolved. Christ alone is the hope for sinful, warring, hating, and hateful mankind. Our hope comes not from Congress, the Supreme Court, or the chief executive. It comes not from a church or "the" church. None is fit to rule the world but the One who was so despised and rejected of men.

Only One has both the right and the power to make peace where there is no peace. Our hope comes from him who lived the life of sacrifice, who died the death of sacrifice, and who ever lives to make intercession for man. Our peace comes from the cross; it comes from the open grave.

What a word is this!

> But all things are of God, who reconciled us to himself through Christ, and gave unto us the ministry of reconciliation; to wit, that God was in Christ reconciling the world unto himself, not reckoning unto them their trespasses, and having committed unto us the word of reconciliation" (2 Corinthians 5:18-19).

He who is our peace has entrusted to us the gospel of peace. In discharging this trust we shall discover how blessed are the peacemakers, for we shall thereby be acknowledged as the sons of God.

Dwight David Eisenhower

President

January 20, 1953—January 20, 1961

2 CHRONICLES 7:14

If my people, who are called by my name, shall humble themselves, and pray, and seek my face, and turn from their wicked ways; then will I hear from heaven, and will forgive their sin, and will heal their land.

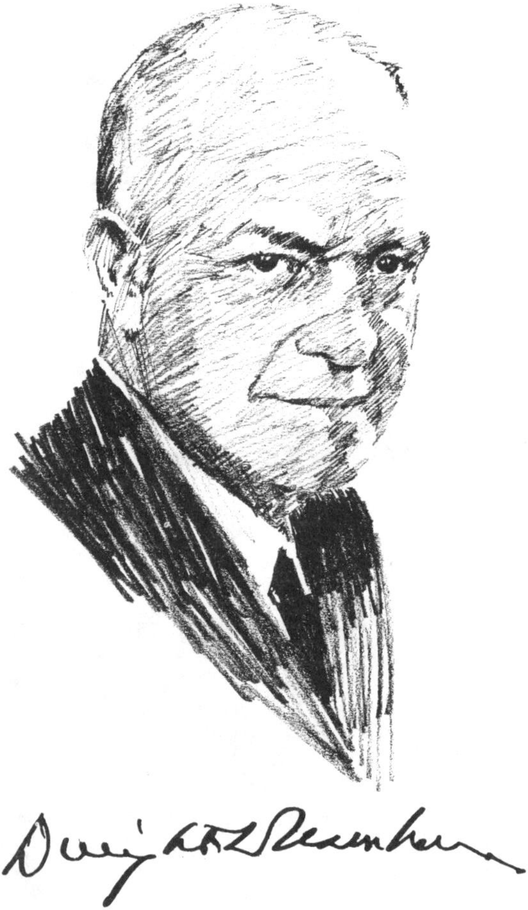

Dwight David Eisenhower

Dwight David Eisenhower was born October 14, 1890, in Denison, Texas, but two years later the family moved to Abilene, Kansas, where he grew up with five brothers. When he finished high school, he went to work in a creamery. But a year later, still hoping to go to college, he took entrance exams for both Annapolis and West Point. He passed both, and in July, 1911, he registered at the Point.

A knee injury forced Eisenhower out of football; at graduation he was ranked as an average student with his best grades in English and history. His first Army assignment was to Fort Sam Houston at San Antonio, Texas, where he met Mamie Geneva Doud. They were married in July, 1916. He served as an instructor in several military camps during World War I and had other assignments until 1926 when he went to the Army General Staff School. There he graduated at the top of the class because of very hard work. Although the years between the wars were not exciting, Eisenhower gained good experience in a number of executive assignments. Just before World War II broke he became a colonel, and in less than two years he was a full general.

The study, the teaching, and the administrative experience of twenty-five Army years prepared Eisenhower for his unique role in World War II. Although he had never commanded a unit in combat, he directed the invasions of French North Africa in 1942, of Sicily and Italy in 1943, and of France in 1944. As supreme commander of all Allied forces in Europe, he managed to get along with and actually lead a diverse body of generals, admirals, and nearly three million troops.

After a hero's welcome back home, Eisenhower served as chief of staff of the Army for more than two years. In 1948 his *Crusade in Europe* was published and became a best seller. He dictated the entire book in seven weeks; he was known in the army as an excellent writer. After two years as president of Columbia University, he was sent back to Europe in 1951 as military head of NATO.

As early as 1943 a few isolated groups were talking about Eisenhower as a possibility for the Presidency. When he retired as chief of staff to go to Columbia in 1947, some national polls showed he could be elected as either a Republican or a Democrat. When he refused to let his name appear as a Republican candidate in the New Hampshire primary, the Democrats thought they had a chance, but he turned down all offers. His name continued in the public mind, and after he revealed early in 1952 that he was a Republican, he became that party's nominee. Eisenhower won the election with a popular vote margin of far more than six million over Adlai E. Stevenson. He served two full terms as the thirty-fourth President of the United States.

Eisenhower's parents were devout Christians, members of the River Brethren, related to Mennonites. After his election he joined a Presbyterian church.

"If My People . . ."

On the morning of his first Inauguration Day, January 20, 1953, Dwight D. Eisenhower went with his family to a communion service at the National Presbyterian Church. Back at the Statler Hotel in a few moments of meditation, he wrote a short prayer which he read before delivering his inaugural address. The middle paragraph pleads:

Give us, we pray, the power to discern clearly right from wrong, and allow all our words and actions to be governed thereby, and by the laws of this land. Especially we pray that our concern shall be for all the people regardless of station, race, or calling.

Back of that expression of trust and yearning was the warm and simple faith of his childhood home, where the Bible was read daily in the family circle. At the urging of his mother, young Dwight read the Bible through twice for himself before going to West Point. When he took the oath of office, his left hand rested on two open Bibles. One had been used by Washington at his first inauguration; the other was a gift to Eisenhower from his mother when he graduated from West Point. It was open at 2 Chronicles 7:14.

This is a favorite text with popular Bible interpreters when dealing with failures of the nation or the threat of some national emergency and the hope of deliverance. Because God was referring to the children of Israel when he responded to Solomon's prayer at the dedication of the new Temple, some want to apply it to the whole American people. But there is a difference, and it shows up in the opening clause: "If my people, who are called by my name . . ."

This verse speaks to *people who bear God's name and acknowledge his authority.* Eisenhower's family had grown up in a devout and dissident Protestant sect which emphasized simple and peaceful living. He once said, "Their Bibles were a live and lusty influence in their lives." He seemed to appreciate being identified with the people of God, and he declared about God's Word: "It has made the mighty humble and has strengthened the weak."

Few people find it easy to "humble themselves." Even those who bear God's name sometimes act like the church belongs to them rather than to the Master. Because they pay the bills, they say they have the right to limit its membership and goals. Some become so enamored of their own interpretations that they resent a different wording given by the Spirit to a fellow believer. All who are called by his name must live under the lordship of Christ. That means much more than *saying* he is Lord; it means obeying his command to love (practice active goodwill), to forgive, and to help. Not our will but his be done.

This inauguration text also says that *when people seek God's presence, they must turn away from evil.* No one can face in opposite directions at the same time. If the children of Israel wanted to pray for God's presence, they must "turn from their wicked ways." People who seek God without admitting their sinfulness and pride have a shallow and imperfect conception of God. To be sure, he is Creator of all things good and beautiful, but he is also the source of righteousness and the judge of all mankind. He has laid moral and ethical demands on all persons.

In a book about Eisenhower's first term, Robert J. Donovan said, "There was no subject on which Eisenhower was more sensitive when he took office than corruption in government."[1] In 1955 when a conflict-of-interest case brought new embarrassment to the administration, Eisenhower said: "I believe it was in [the fall of 1952] I tried to explain my conception of what a public servant owed to the government . . . that his actions had to be impeccable, both from the standpoint of law [and] from the standpoint of ethics."[2] Because he felt that government service was not a right but a privilege, the conduct of officials must be beyond reproach.

Being aware of hatred, envy, prejudice, or infidelity in oneself or in another is not the sign of a guilt complex or some emotional imbalance. It may well be the first step toward spiritual health. Admitting one's fault and turning away from it is part of what conversion is all about. It sets the stage for a redemptive encounter with God in Christ.

A third truth revealed in the verse chosen by President Eisenhower is that *God is ready to restore broken relationships.* He awaits only genuine repentance and the desire for reinstatement. The person who carries God's name and wants to be in his family will feel crushed when he realizes that his pride or greed has blocked his relationship with God. Whatever may have been the deed, he is assured that God will "hear . . . forgive . . . and heal." That is based on God's mercy and a person's true repentance.

Although Eisenhower was a military man and during wartime expressed himself with hardness toward the enemy, he was also a President of patience and restraint, believing in law, and always hoping that disagreements could be settled "with intellect and decent purpose." His personal bearing and his style of leadership produced, in Donovan's words, "perhaps the most important of Eisenhower's achievements as President—his guidance of the people away from the hatred, the suspicions, the lies, the bitterness, the savagery even that had defiled American public life since the end of World War II."[3]

No man can play God without fostering idolatry, but leaders of integrity and godly character can encourage some of the people to "turn from their wicked ways" and seek the presence of God.

Eisenhower was seventy at the end of his second term, and he used radio and television for a farewell address to the nation. It contained both warning and hope. He regretted the need for vast expenditures of the military establishment through the large arms industry:

"In the councils of government, we must guard against the acquisition of unwarranted influence, whether sought or unsought, by the military-industrial complex. . .

"We must never let the weight of this combination endanger our liberties or democratic processes. . ."

He also warned against the "danger that public policy could itself become the captive of a scientific-technological elite." Although some progress had been made toward world peace, he was not satisfied. But he was hopeful as he said: "Down the long lane of the history yet to be written America knows that this world of ours, ever growing smaller, must avoid becoming a community of dreadful fear and hate, and be, instead, a proud confederation of trust and respect."

---

1. Robert J. Donovan, *Eisenhower, The Inside Story* (New York: Harper & Row, 1956), p. 79.
2. Ibid. p. 334.
3. Ibid.

John Fitzgerald Kennedy

President

January 20, 1961—November 22, 1963

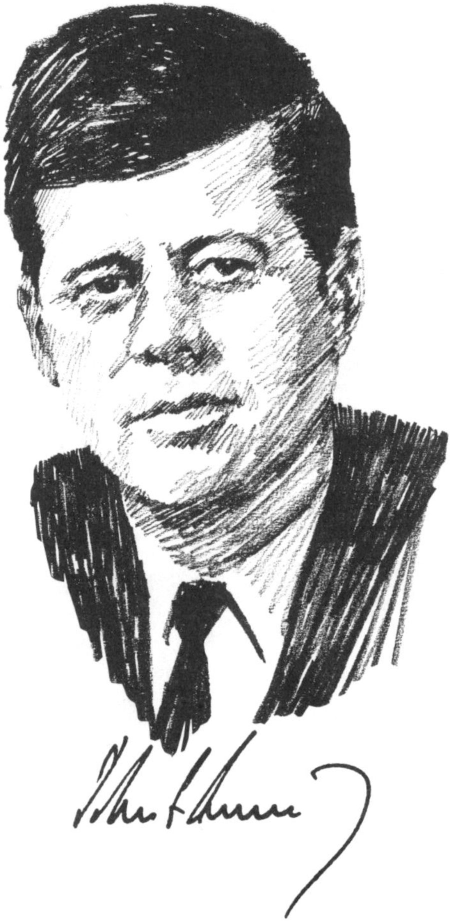

JOHN FITZGERALD KENNEDY

John Fitzgerald Kennedy was born, May 29, 1917, in Brookline, Massachusetts, the second of nine children of Joseph and Rose Kennedy. Both sides of the family had been prominent in politics, and after World War I Joseph Kennedy started building a major fortune. In 1937 President Roosevelt made him United States Ambassador to Great Britain.

While Jack was in elementary school, the family moved to New York City, and he attended several private schools. Although not an outstanding student or athlete, when he graduated from Choate School he was voted most likely to succeed. In his last year at Harvard he became interested in economics and political science. His thesis on "Appeasement at Munich" was commended, and he turned it into a book, *Why England Slept,* which became a best seller in 1940.

Early in 1941 Jack Kennedy interrupted graduate study for military service. An old back injury kept him out of the Army, but following months of strenuous exercise he was accepted by the Navy. Assignment to active duty was delayed, but after PT-boat training he was given command in March, 1943, of a torpedo boat in the South Pacific. After thirty successful missions, the boat was on night patrol early in August when it was cut in half by a Japanese destroyer. Two of the men were killed, but several days later the others were rescued largely by the effort of Lieutenant Kennedy. In 1944 he had an operation on his spine and was convalescing when the news came that his older brother, Joe, had been killed while on a bombing flight in Europe.

Because the Kennedy family had wanted Joe to go into politics, Jack began thinking along that line after he was discharged in 1945. He moved his residence to Boston and began working toward Democratic nomination for Congress in 1946. He learned a great deal in that first campaign, and his family and friends gave enthusiastic support. He won that election and did it again in 1948 and 1950.

In 1952 Kennedy decided to run for the Senate against Henry Cabot Lodge, a liberal Republican who had served since 1936. Again, with family money and personal help, Kennedy won although Massachusetts elected a Republican governor and went big for Eisenhower. Kennedy continued to work hard for his state and liberal causes for the country. In September, 1953, he married Jacqueline Lee Bouvier. In October, 1954, he had another operation on his spine and a third in February. During his long convalescence he wrote *Profiles in Courage,* which was published in 1956, became a best seller, and was awarded the Pulitzer Prize for biography. When re-elected to the Senate in 1958, he was one of the best-known men in the country.

From that year Kennedy and his family were looking toward the Presidency. Primaries in Wisconsin and West Virginia in 1960 led to his Democratic nomination on the first ballot. During the campaign he faced opposition because of his age (only 43), because he was a Roman Catholic, and because the Republicans had selected incumbent Vice-President Nixon as their candidate. In four TV debates—the first in history—the candidates discussed their views before the nation. Kennedy won by a very close margin, only 112,000 popular votes.

On Delivering the Oppressed

January 20, 1961 was a bright, cold day in Washington, D.C. A heavy snowstorm had blanketed the seaboard, and transportation was almost paralyzed, but a large crowd gathered in the plaza before the Capitol for the inauguration of the nation's thirty-fifth President. With his left hand on a closed family copy of the Douay Bible, John F. Kennedy took his oath of office before Chief Justice Earl Warren. Then he delivered a crisp and memorable inaugural address.

Its first sentence called the occasion "a celebration of freedom," and its fourth paragraph promised "to oppose any foe to assure the survival and the success of liberty." It was addressed to young listeners to kindle fresh commitment to the high, historic goals of the nation. Although President Kennedy did not select an inaugural text as had most of his predecessors, he did quote part of a verse from Isaiah to sound again the favorite chord of freedom. Addressing "those nations who would make themselves our adversary," he urged both sides to explore the problems and offer serious proposals for their solution and finally to unite in trying to obey the command of Isaiah to "undo the heavy burdens, and to let the oppressed go free" (58:6, KJV).

Isaiah was speaking to the exiles who had returned home. They were observing a fast, probably one of four added during the exile to commemorate the fall of Jerusalem. It was supposed to represent an inner attitude, but the prophet sensed its hypocrisy. In verse 3 the people had complained that they received no reward for fasting, that God seemed to pay no attention to their pious diligence. The prophet replied in God's behalf. Their fasting made no change in their treatment of one another; it often bred quarreling even when they put on a sacred show.

Instead of all that sham, the kind of fast God preferred was deeds of compassion and generosity toward enslaved people. The "bands of wickedness" in verse 6 may refer to the cruel treatment of those who had to become slaves to pay off their debts. Other phrases probably refer to the ordeal of poverty. All in that community were children of Israel, but some were comfortable and cruel while others were hungry and hopeless. Through Isaiah, God was saying that freedom for the oppressed was more important than pious fasting.

This verse is saying three things to us. First, *it recognizes that some people are free and others are enslaved.* Apparently, the prophet was talking about an economic and legal situation. A similar condition in the United States probably influenced President Kennedy to be concerned for freedom. Ever since the Supreme Court decision in 1954 against racial segregation in public schools, pressure had been mounting for the full application of that decision and for other legal deliverances of black citizens. A young, black Baptist pastor led a bus boycott in Montgomery, Alabama, to wipe out segregated seating, and Martin Luther King, Jr., became the spiritual leader of the black freedom movement. Free people began to realize that a large part of the population was economically and socially fettered.

From abroad came news of recurring communist efforts to destroy freedom in Southeast Asia and Cuba. Many remembered sadly the pictures of Russian tanks crushing the 1956 revolt in Hungary. Freedom-loving Americans resented governments which forbade free speech, assembly, religion, and the vote. The new President was keenly aware that both freedom and its lack were in the world together.

Isaiah's verse reveals another truth: *it declares God's concern for those who are bound.* Man was not created to be a slave, despite the cruel practice of mighty empires. President Kennedy in his inaugural address called it a revolutionary belief "that the rights of man come not from the generosity of the state but from the hand of God." One man enslaving another, therefore, is a violation of God's intention; he wants to see "the oppressed go free."

President Kennedy did not talk about his faith or religious practices; in his speeches he cited more often the thoughts of past Presidents than words from the Bible. But his mother's life centered in her church, and Kennedy was forthrightly committed to it also. His integrity as a believer must have appealed to many Protestant voters. Certainly, the urgency of his commitment to freedom seemed to stem from his view of God.

We can make a third affirmation about Isaiah 58:6: *it insists that those who are free are obligated to deliver those who are bound.* In a special message to Congress, March 1, 1961, President Kennedy proposed the establishment of a Peace Corps which would enlist well-trained young men and women for people-to-people service abroad. Their skills in teaching, agriculture, and public health would be offered to countries which needed them. The workers would receive no salary, only transportation and basic expenses. As much as possible, they would try to identify with the people and always demonstrate a spirit of helpfulness. The Peace Corps became a notable achievement of Kennedy's administration. It proved his conviction that the free are obligated to help liberate others.

Kennedy's favorite quotation was from Edmund Burke, Irish-born English statesman of the late eighteenth century: "The only thing necessary for the triumph of evil is for good men to do nothing." This is also the way freedom is lost or never gained. Civil rights legislation of 1957 had started to implement Court decisions against racial discrimination. Drastic action was taken several times during the Kennedy administration to enforce the law and protect black people who were trying to live by it. In a television address the President said that the grandsons of the freed slaves of the previous century "are not yet freed from social and economic oppression, and this nation, for all its hopes and all its boasts, will not be fully free until all its citizens are free."

Perhaps the best remembered sentence of that inaugural address was: "And so my fellow Americans, ask not what your country can do for you; ask what you can do for your country." These were words from a young man, full of zest and hope. But the last sentence is also memorable, revealing a man of realistic faith: ". . . let us go forth to lead the land we love, asking His blessing and His help, but knowing that here on earth God's work must truly be our own."

On November 22, 1963, President Kennedy was assassinated as his motorcade drive through downtown Dallas, Texas. While millions of shocked and grieving Americans watched on television, he was buried, November 25, in Arlington National Cemetery.

Lyndon Baines Johnson

President

November 22, 1963—January 20, 1969

2 CHRONICLES 1:10

Give me now wisdom and knowledge, that I may go out and come in before this people; for who can judge this thy people, that is so great?

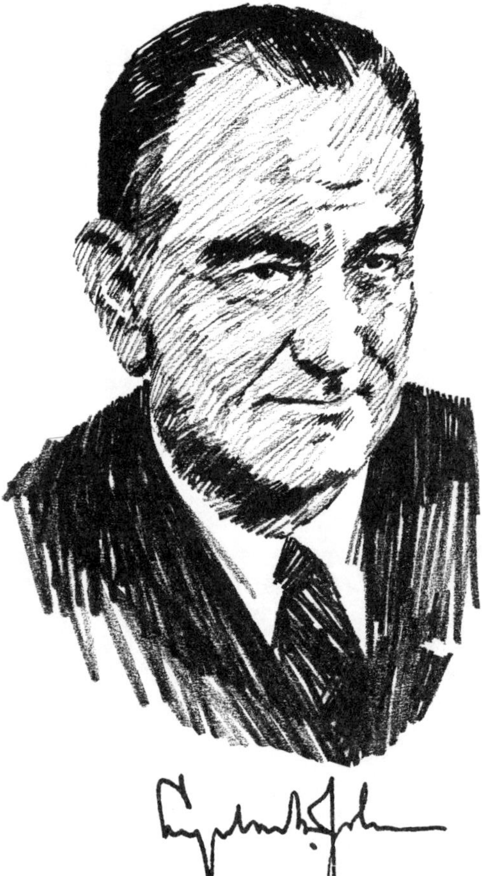

Lyndon Baines Johnson

Lyndon Baines Johnson was born near Stonewall, Texas, August 27, 1908, the first of five children to Samuel and Rebekah Johnson. In 1913 the family moved to Johnson City, named for Lyndon's grandfather, about fifty miles due west of Austin. Both grandfathers had been members of the Texas Legislature, and before Lyndon reached his teen years, his father was serving in that body. So he grew up with an unusual awareness of the world of politics.

When Lyndon graduated from high school as president of his class, instead of following his mother's urging to go to college, he hitchhiked to California with some friends. In less than a year he was glad to get back to Johnson City and work on a road gang. After about two years he enrolled at Southwest State Teachers College in San Marcos and worked his way to graduation in 1930.

During a year of teaching public speaking and debate in a Houston high school, Johnson became quite interested in the problems and potential of the Mexican-American minority. After wealthy Richard M. Kleberg was elected to Congress, the rancher-legislator employed Lyndon Johnson as his secretary in Washington. From 1932 to 1935 Johnson made it possible for Kleberg to do a lot for his congressional district and for Johnson to learn how Congress worked. In November, 1934, just two months after they had met, Lyndon married Claudia Alta Taylor, nicknamed Lady Bird. In 1935 President Roosevelt appointed him National Youth Administration director for

Texas, and he found jobs for thousands of young people.

When Congressman James Buchanan of the Tenth Congressional district died in 1937, Johnson was one of ten candidates in the election to fill the vacancy. Because he supported Roosevelt completely, the other nine campaigned against Johnson, but young voters and hard work won the election. He was reelected in 1938, 1940, and 1942. While in the House he pushed rural electrification, public housing, and a strong Navy. A few days after Pearl Harbor, Johnson volunteered for active duty and was sent to the South Pacific for a few months.

In 1948 Johnson and ten other candidates ran for Democratic nomination for a seat in the Senate. In the run-off primary Johnson won by 87 votes over Governor Coke Stevenson. The slight but victorious edge came from the Mexican-Americans in the southern counties. Although a freshman Senator, Johnson's leadership was recognized at once, and by 1951 he was elected Democratic whip and two years later, floor leader, the youngest ever in the Senate. Largely by his efforts, Senate Democrats supported President Eisenhower on many issues opposed by conservative Senate Republicans. On both sides of the aisle he was recognized as having ability and power. He was reelected in 1954.

Lyndon Johnson hoped in 1960 he would be the Democratic presidential nominee, but Kennedy won, and Johnson accepted the invitation to be his running mate. Johnson strengthened the ticket, and after they were elected, President Kennedy gave Johnson unusual responsibilities.

On November 22, 1963, less than two hours after President Kennedy was killed in Dallas, Texas, Johnson was sworn in as the thirty-sixth President of the United States.

A Prayer for Wisdom

Within a few minutes after President Kennedy's casket had been brought on board Air Force One, Lyndon Baines Johnson was sworn in on the plane as President. While his left hand rested on a Bible used by Kennedy, he repeated the oath as stated by Federal Judge Sarah T. Hughes, the first woman ever to perform that task. His first presidential command was, "All right, let's get this plane back to Washington." A few hours later at Andrews Field, Johnson faced a crowd of mourners and thousands on radio and television and phrased his grief in four sentences; then he added: "I will do my best. That is all I can do. I ask for your help and God's."

Many people who heard that earnest request were not surprised to learn fourteen months later that for his first inauguration President Johnson selected 2 Chronicles 1:10 as his text. During the morning of January 21, 1965, the family and many friends went to an interfaith prayer service at the National City Christian Church. The President was a Disciple, a member of the Christian Church, while Mrs. Johnson was an Episcopalian. The Bible she held (at his request) was a 1952 Christmas gift from the President's mother.

Johnson had been elected by one of the greatest landslides in American history. The people made quite clear their choice between him and Senator Barry Goldwater. Evidently they liked what Johnson had been doing since that tragic day in Dallas. Although some opposed aspects of his domestic program, the 1964 polls showed 70 to 80 percent of the people thought he was doing a good job. Perhaps this approval heightened his sense of the awesome responsibility of the presidency.

Although Solomon had carried some responsibility during David's last days, when his father died, Solomon realized that the weighty crown was his alone. On one occasion he and a host of the people went to Gibeon to offer sacrifices on Bezaleel's brazen altar. During the night the king had a vision; God offered to give him whatever he asked. Solomon's immediate petition was for "wisdom and knowledge" to lead the people and judge them. God commended him for not requesting wealth, honor, or long life, and he promised to grant his prayer and give him the other things besides.

Solomon's prayer showed, first, that *he recognized his responsibility.* He was young and inexperienced, but he had seen in his father David some of the things a king was supposed to do. He must "go out and come in before this people" as the warrior-king, leading the army. But more important, he must "judge this thy people"—rule with competence and justice. His new role was a job to be done with the people and in the presence of God.

That was the mood of the new President Johnson at Andrews Field when he said, "I ask for your help and God's." Because of his twelve years in the House of Representatives and eleven years in the Senate, he knew a great deal about government and its relation to the people. After Eisenhower became President in 1953, Johnson became minority leader in the Senate. He urged his colleagues: "When we are forced by our convictions to oppose Administration proposals, our opposition will be based on principle and will be expressed in a principled manner." He called this the "politics of responsibility." As a lawmaker he liked to call a meeting of opponents and say, "Let us reason together." As President, he was often painfully aware of opposing forces and viewpoints, and the responsibility of his office weighed heavily upon him.

In the second place, as Solomon prayed *he recognized his need*. He had grown up in the palace and had been chosen by David as his successor, but Solomon knew all this was not enough to answer the hard questions that would arise in the nation's life. So he prayed for "an understanding heart" (1 Kings 3:9), which means the practical wisdom needed to make right decisions.

On January 8, 1964, President Johnson delivered his first State of the Union address and urged Congress to fulfill Kennedy's program: more action for civil rights, all-out war on poverty and unemployment, a medical care program for the aged, an effective foreign aid program, and other goals. As majority leader in the Senate, he had pushed the civil rights acts of 1957 and 1960. Now as President he saw these needs and their achievement in a different light. He had learned well how to work in the legislative halls; now he must discover the techniques of the executive.

Johnson's inauguration in 1965 partly filled one of his great needs. During the year after the assassination, he felt overshadowed by the Kennedy mystique. He was also perhaps unconsciously defensive about his "Southern image." So, the stunning election in November showed that the people *wanted* him as President in his own right. Public opinion polls continued to run high in his favor, and many aspects of his Great Society domestic program were accepted by Congress.

Solomon's prayer revealed his sense of responsibility as the leader of his people and his sense of deep need, but it also *acknowledged God as the source of his help*. What else would be expected of David's son and the one chosen to build the first temple? It was a high moment for the young king, but other loyalties were waiting to contest it.

President Johnson did not parade his Christian commitment, but that simple appeal, "I ask for your help and God's" was earnest and sincere. At a Presidential Prayer Breakfast he once said, "Since the United States first stood on its feet among the nations of the earth, the men who have guided her destiny have had the strength for their tasks by going to their knees."

While the domestic achievements of President Johnson will be appreciated, things went sour in the area of foreign relations. At first the country had supported American involvement in Vietnam, but as the struggle dragged on with little hope of solution, the people took sides for either an all-out effort for victory or complete withdrawal. As war deaths mounted into the thousands and demonstrations increased against the draft, the national attitude changed. Eventually the frustration, disillusionment, and resentment seemed to focus on the President. Approval of his policies dropped to 39 percent in 1967. Johnson declared: "A President's hardest task is not to do what is right, but to know what is right."

On March 31, 1968, President Johnson told a nationwide television audience: "I shall not seek—and will not accept—the nomination of my party for another term as your President." On January 20, 1969 he told the new President Richard Nixon, "This is the happiest day of my life." He retired to his ranch on the Pedernales at Johnson City, Texas, and died there on January 22, 1973.

Richard Milhous Nixon

President

January 20, 1969—August 9, 1974

ISAIAH 2:4

And he will judge between the nations, and will decide concerning many peoples; and they shall beat their swords into plowshares, and their spears into pruning-hooks; nation shall not lift up sword against nation, neither shall they learn war any more.

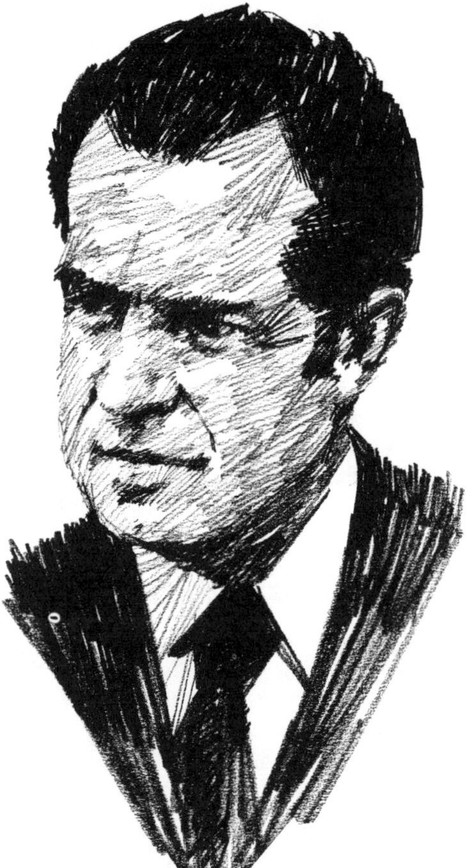

RICHARD MILHOUS NIXON

Richard Milhous Nixon was born January 9, 1913 in Yorba Linda, California, the second of five sons of Francis Anthony and Hannah Milhous Nixon. His father had worked at many jobs and managed to keep the family fed and clothed. In 1922 they moved to the Quaker town of Whittier, where Richard was a good student and became a star debater in high school and maintained that pattern through Whittier College. Richard won a scholarship to the new Duke University Law School.

After graduation Dick Nixon passed the California Bar Exam and began practicing with Whittier's oldest firm in 1937. He met Thelma "Pat" Ryan at a Little Theatre tryout and proposed that very night. She finally said yes in the spring of 1940, and they were married on June 21. After Pearl Harbor the Quaker Nixon enlisted in the Navy and served in the South Pacific. He was discharged in 1945 as a lieutenant commander.

Even before he returned to Whittier, he was called by a committee to be the Republican nominee who would attempt to unseat five-term Jerry Voorhis as Congressman from the 12th District. Open debates, hard work, and Dick's exploitation of an endorsement of Voorhis by the Political Action Committee won the race. During his four years, 1947-50, in the House, Nixon served on the Education and Labor Committee and the House Un-American Activities Committee. He gained national prominence on the latter committee in the Whittaker Chambers-Alger Hiss hearings.

In 1950 Nixon ran against Mrs. Helen Gahagan Douglas for

the Senate. It was a rough campaign on both sides, but controversial Nixon tactics won the race. As a successful vote-getter and speaker, he was asked by General Eisenhower to be his running-mate in the Presidential campaign of 1952. Despite the revelation of a "secret" political fund for Nixon in California, he made a nationwide television speech explaining it in such a way as to convince millions of voters.

President Eisenhower had promised Nixon that the Vice-Presidency would be a meaningful job, and he gave him several important assignments. During that first term Nixon assumed the task of maintaining Republican unity while the extremism of Senator Joe McCarthy was threatening it. Despite some opposition, Nixon was renominated in 1956 for Eisenhower's re-election campaign. During that term Nixon was the President's emissary to several foreign countries, and his visits in Venezuela and Russia were especially significant.

In 1960 Nixon was the Republican presidential candidate, but after a rugged campaign he lost to John F. Kennedy by the smallest percentage margin in any presidential election. Then in 1962, hoping to retain his role in party leadership, Nixon ran for governor of California but lost to the incumbent Pat Brown. In 1963 he moved to New York City and joined a successful law firm. He was soon considered the chief partner. In 1964 he campaigned vigorously for Barry Goldwater and for Congressional candidates in 1966.

A Gallup poll in 1967 showed that 68 percent of Republican county chairmen across the country favored Nixon as the 1968 candidate. In a very close race, the so-called "New Nixon" won over Hubert Humphrey, vice-president under Johnson, and it was called the greatest political comeback in American history.

A Longing for Peace

When Richard Milhous Nixon, thirty-seventh President of the United States, stood to take the oath of office, January 20, 1969, his wife held two Bibles that had been in their families for many years, and his left hand touched Isaiah 2:4. It was a cold, gray day, and forbidding national problems—Vietnam, inflation, and racial tension—waited briefly in the wings, as it were, until the drama of inauguration ended. At least two of those problems needed the message of that inaugural text.

For centuries the picturesque language—"they shall beat their swords into plowshares, and their spears into pruning-hooks"—had quickened the longings of men of many nations. Even when they saw little real possibility of peace in their time, they still hoped that it might come, at least for their children. Orators—both religious and political—had quoted the verse without really confronting the meaning or cost of peace. It comes too easily to modern lips because we no longer fight with swords and spears. But the verse is there in the Word, still beckoning those who believe in God, still daring men and women to hope and work for peace.

The prophet, probably writing near the end of his career, may have looked back on many years of international strife and bloodshed. He remembered the suffering, the greed, and the hopelessness of it all. Then God gave him insight into the divine will, and he saw God's purpose in his people extending to "all nations." In a time yet to come the "Lord's house" would draw them to learn "his ways" and together they would "walk in his paths." They would not go to Jerusalem to sacrifice but to receive the law and the "word of the Lord."

Verse 4 pictures the Lord as judging among the nations; as God of the whole world he has that right. He would sit in judgment on those who threatened Judah's life and safety. As differences and quarrels arose, he would help men see what was right and wrong. By means of his law and word, they would perceive relationships and obligations which their old idolatries had denied or perverted. His teaching would undermine their value structure of "might makes right" and similar mottoes of selfishness and greed.

Only as this new way of life permeates the mind and mood of the nations can Isaiah's great word picture of swords and spears come true. Who needs a sword when fear and suspicion are gone? Who needs a spear when there are no enemies? Then the sharp edge can better turn the earth for food, and the long-handled blade improve both vine and tree. How that judgment of God among the nations would alter *our* country's budget! What a difference it would make also for those who fear *us!* But what good thing could be done with an M-1 rifle or an ICBM? With real trust in one another, the world's peoples could change these tools of hideous death into food, medicine, schools, and other elements of the good life.

Although Isaiah did not promise there would be no misunderstandings between nations, he did say they would not "learn war any more." War is not inevitable, is not inherent in competitive human relations. It is the vicious denial of those relations, the reversion to savagery. Isaiah yearned for the time when nations of our time would be ignorant of napalm, defoliation, and unconditional surrender. Only a God above all nationalism could give the prophet a vision like that.

No one knows what President Nixon had in mind when he selected this verse for his inauguration. Many people probably thought it was both motto and goal for the new Administration. American involvement in Vietnam had begun in 1955, and the first loss of life came in December, 1961. Then the Gulf of Tonkin Resolution in 1964 had opened the way for expanding military support. Four years later strong anti-war demonstrations reacted to the half-million fighting force and multibillion-dollar expenditures. Although peace talks began that year, both sides seemed to be looking for victory rather than peace. President Nixon began a withdrawal of troops in 1969; but in 1970 the enemy was bombed in Cambodia and Nixon declared on television: "We will not be humiliated. We will not be defeated." Opposition to the war grew with huge demonstrations—some peaceful and some violent. Peace talks with the North Vietnamese had started in 1968; they were suspended in 1972.

In that election year President Nixon made a dramatic effort at international understanding by visiting both communist China and Russia. At his second inauguration, President Nixon promised to trim down various Federal social programs, but later the proposed military budget was increased by $5.6 billion. Finally on January 27, 1973 the warring parties signed the "Agreement on Ending the War and Restoring Peace in Vietnam." But real peace never came.

A few days later Judge John J. Sirica charged that the Watergate trial had not answered some important questions. In that trial six men had been convicted on various charges of breaking into and bugging the Democratic National headquarters in Washington's Watergate apartment complex in 1972. A Senate panel began hearings in May and continued until early August. Key White House staff members resigned, and the President offered various explanations to the press as the hearings continued. The initial crime paled before the devious involvements of the cover-up. By April some things seemed to indicate that the President knew more than he was saying. In October after he fired the special prosecutor he had appointed to get to the bottom of Watergate, an impeachment resolution was introduced in the House of Representatives. The Judiciary Committee began its meetings and by July, 1974 had agreed on three articles of impeachment. Taped conversations in the White House revealed that the President was involved in the cover-up from the beginning.

On August 8, President Nixon announced his resignation from office.

Gerald Rudolph Ford

President

August 9, 1974—January 20, 1977

PROVERBS 3:5-6

Trust in Jehovah with all thy heart, and lean not upon thine own understanding: in all thy ways acknowledge him, and he will direct thy paths.

Gerald R. Ford

Gerald Rudolph Ford

Gerald Rudolph Ford, Jr. was born July 14, 1913, in Omaha, Nebraska, but he grew up in Grand Rapids, Michigan. His father did not prosper as a businessman, but he was noted for character and good works. Jerry carried his high school enthusiasm for football to the University of Michigan and played center on the undefeated national champions of 1932 and 1933. He worked his way through Yale Law School by coaching football and boxing.

After graduation in 1941 he started practicing law in Grand Rapids. Then he enlisted in the Navy the next year and was an instructor until he was assigned to the aircraft carrier *Monterey* for duty in the South Pacific. When he came out in January, 1946, as a lieutenant commander, he returned to practice law in Grand Rapids.

Two years later Senator Arthur Vandenberg encouraged Jerry to run for Congress, and he won with 60 percent of the vote. On October 15 he married Elizabeth Bloomer, who had helped in his campaign. They moved to Washington, and Ford was reelected twelve times. He stayed in close touch with his Fifth District, making frequent visits and trying to respond to all who needed his help. In 1965 he became Republican minority leader in the House, and the next year he and Senator Everett Dirksen staged "The Ev and Jerry Show" for television to explain Republican positions on the administration of President Johnson.

Congressman Ford was completely loyal to President Nixon

and the programs he advocated. He was friendly, always fair and honest, and a hard worker. In the fall of 1973 charges of bribery were being gathered against Vice-President Spiro T. Agnew from his days as governor of Maryland. When he pleaded no contest against a Federal charge of filing a false income tax return in 1967—thereby admitting his guilt—he resigned from the Vice-Presidency, October 12. Nixon had selected Gerald Ford to take his place. Confirmation hearings by the House Judiciary Committee lasted six days, but 350 FBI agents had found nothing to prevent House approval of Ford.

In the following months Vice-President Ford made hundreds of appearances across the country trying to improve the image of the Administration while inflation and Watergate were undermining confidence. But finally on August 5 President Nixon admitted that he knew about the Watergate break-in six days after it happened and tried to cover it up. That revelation led Republican members of the House Judiciary Committee to say they would vote for impeachment. Faced with almost certain conviction, President Nixon announced his retirement.

Within two hours after Nixon had left the White House on August 9, 1974, Gerald Ford was sworn in as the thirty-eighth President of the United States. One of his first actions was to pardon Nixon for any criminal involvement in the Watergate activity or cover-up. During his brief tenure, President Ford restored openness and candor to the White House, but his relations with the largely Democratic Congress were not productive. In 1976, however, he won the Republican nomination over former Governor Ronald Reagan of California but lost the election to Jimmy Carter. Although President Ford left the Washington scene for a new home in California, he did not give up his political interests.

Trusting God's Guidance

On August 9, 1974 about 250 guests filled the East Room of the White House for the inauguration of Gerald Rudolph Ford, as thirty-eighth President of the United States. As Chief Justice Warren Burger administered the oath, Mrs. Ford held their son's open Bible for the President's left hand. It was open at Proverbs 3:5-6 which this devout Episcopalian uses each night as a prayer. Rather than a petition, it is a personal reminder of the essential relationship of the believer with his God.

The book of Proverbs was probably a book of moral and religious instruction for young Jewish men, but its wisdom is still applicable to all who believe. The first three verses of chapter 3 urge the reader to remember God's law, mercy, and truth. "Remember" is a key concept in Judaism; strength and guidance for today come as believers remember what God has done in the past. In keeping his remembered laws, a person will be given long life and peace.

Verses 5 and 6 turn the introspection of remembering the past into the commitment and action of today. The God of Abraham and Moses fulfilled his promises and required righteousness in his people in every era. God did not change. Thus, the believer is urged to trust him completely. Accept him as Father-God; measure your life by his pattern; look to his Word for guidance in decisions and strength in times of testing. "Do not rely on your own insight." Whatever information you may bring to a problem, let the final decision depend clearly on your trust in God.

One important word of these two verses is "all," referring to all of one's heart and all of one's ways. Both times it calls for a person's complete commitment. Failing to live up to that "allness" prevents many people from enjoying God's guidance. Without his help our ways are crooked and obscure.

The mood of this text was reflected in President Ford's inaugural speech. *Time* said it was "refreshingly candid, sincere, unpretentious and effectively crafted to ease national tension and clear the air of Watergate." He acknowledged that he had not been *elected* as President, but he asked the people "to confirm me as your President with your prayers." In closing, he referred to his earlier promise "to uphold the Constitution, to do what is right as God gives me to see the right, and to do the very best I can for America." Then he added: "God helping me, I will not let you down."

Because of the essential differences between the legislative and executive branches of government, no one could predict the style of Gerald Ford in his new role. But they expected him to maintain a healthy openness with the press and draw on his past experience in his relations with Congress. Once in discussing his way of doing things, Ford had said, "You have to give a little, take a little, to get what you really want, but you don't give up your principles." The general cast of those principles for him may be caught in this statement of January, 1974: "It's the quality of the ordinary, the straight, the square that accounts for the great stability and success of our nation. It's a quality to be proud of. But it's a quality many people seem to have neglected."

Without making any show of his religious commitment but ready to accept a heavy responsibility in behalf of his country, here was a President who entrusted his skills to the guidance of God.

Jimmy Carter

President

January 20, 1977—

MICAH 6:8

He hath showed thee, O man, what is good; and what doth Jehovah require of thee, but to do justly, and to love kindness and to walk humbly with thy God?

Jimmy Carter

Jimmy Carter

James Earl Carter, Jr., was born October 1, 1924 near Plains, Georgia, the first child of James Earl and Lillian Carter. His father managed a grocery store and owned the town icehouse and dry cleaning establishment. Later he sold farm supplies and helped farmers sell their peanuts. He was much involved in community life and eventually served in the Georgia legislature. Jimmy's mother, "Miz Lillian" as she is popularly known, was a nurse and took cases frequently while her family was growing up. When she was sixty-eight years old, she was accepted for Peace Corps service in India for two years.

Jimmy finished high school at sixteen and studied one year at Georgia Southwestern College in Americus. Because from his early teens he had been interested in a naval career, however, he took science and math at Georgia Tech for a year before going on to the United States Naval Academy. After graduation in 1946, he returned home and married Rosalynn Smith.

After two years of battleship duty out of Norfolk, Jimmy was accepted for the submarine school and service. Then followed a series of family separations and reunions for five years in Honolulu, San Diego, New London, and finally Schenectady. That last assignment involved working with Admiral Rickover in developing the atomic submarine.

When Jimmy's father died in 1953, however, he felt so keenly that he was needed at home that he resigned from the Navy, even over Rosalynn's protest. That first year of farming was hard, and the next year he was refused a bank loan, but in a few years Jimmy was making a good living. At the same time he became involved in community life: the church, county school board, Lion's Club, and eventually a county planning and development board. After the famous 1954 Supreme Court decision on integration, Jimmy Carter revealed several times how he felt about traditional race relations. These and other factors quickened his interest in politics.

In 1962, Jimmy ran for the Georgia Senate and lost by a few votes. But one poll watcher reported something he had seen, and that led to an investigation which eventually ended with a fraudulent box being thrown out and Jimmy being declared the winner. In 1966, he ran for governor when the leading Democratic candidate withdrew for health reasons, but Lester Maddox won the nomination. Although the defeat jolted him, Jimmy began almost at once to plan for the 1970 campaign, and with clever strategy and hard work, he won it. During his four years, he made significant improvements in state government, brought many black people into the political picture, and firmed up his convictions in behalf of the whole country.

Late in 1974 the news got out that Jimmy Carter was planning to run for the Presidency of the United States. State-by-state organization was soon underway, polls were taken, and speeches were made. He ran in all but one Democratic primary and won most of them, displacing fifteen hopefuls and favorite sons. Despite that dramatic victory for a hard-working but relatively unknown candidate, the polls began to show strong gains by President Ford. Carter seemed to gain an edge in three televised debates, but the election was not finally settled until after that decisive November midnight with projected electoral votes totaling 297 for Carter and 241 for Ford.

Not Ritual but Righteousness

When Jimmy Carter was inaugurated the thirty-ninth President on January 20, 1977, his Bible, a gift from his mother, was open at Micah 6:8, and he noted that fact in his speech. It was a natural comment for a man who describes himself as a born-again Christian—a Southern Baptist with experience as a Sunday School teacher and a deacon. For him the Bible speaks with authority for faith and conduct.

The verse from Micah is one of the best-known verses in the Old Testament. Although it ends with a question mark, it is a positive declaration by the prophet of what the Lord required of his people. In verses 6-7 the prophet had written as a representative of the people. They thought that an elaborate ritual of sacrifices was needed to win the Lord's favor. Verse 6 describes customary worship. If that is not adequate, should they multiply their sacrifices by the thousands? Or should they resort even to human sacrifice?

Patiently, Micah responded: the Lord has already made it clear what he expected from believers. Not ostentatious worship but right living. He wanted them to *practice justice* in righting wrongs, in living by God's law, and in being honest and fair with their neighbors. Ceremonial worship is not wrong, but it is irrelevant when worshipers ignore justice.

Jimmy Carter was sensitive to this godly expectation when he refused to join the White Citizens' Council in his community, even when told that all other white men had signed up. It came again when he and his family and one other member of the church were the only ones to vote to allow black people to worship with the white congregation. Later, when he was inaugurated governor of Georgia, he declared: "I say to you quite frankly that the time for racial discrimination is over. Our people have already made this major and difficult decision, but we cannot underestimate the challenge of hundreds of minor decisions yet to be made. Our inherent human charity and our religious beliefs will be taxed to the limit. No poor, rural, weak, or black person should ever have to bear the additional burden of being deprived of the opportunity of an education, a job or simple justice."

Closely related to practicing justice is the Lord's second requirement: *love kindness.* That is, practice active goodwill in dealing with all people. In God's sight, justice is not enough in relations between persons, even as human beings desperately need mercy from the Judge of all the earth. Despite their messages of judgment, the prophets—including Micah—knew the mercy and kindness of the Lord. Then from the life and teachings of Jesus, the New Testament affirmed: "God is love."

President Carter's first official action was to pardon the Vietnam draft evaders. Since that war had seriously divided the country, with prominent and sincere people on both sides, the pardon was vehemently attacked as being both too soft and too hard. But anyone who tries to practice kindness can expect this kind of criticism.

One interpreter of Jimmy Carter was impressed by his Law Day address at the University of Georgia, May 4, 1974. He was talking to lawyers and public officials, and trying to say what needed to be done in Georgia for the sake of justice. He acknowledged his lack of expertise in the legal field, but he was talking about what persons can do for persons and about the selfish resistance to change that blocks that kind of action. The interpreter, Tom Collins, concluded from that speech that Jimmy Carter is a man "rooted and grounded in compassion."[1]

Micah mentioned one other requirement by which God measured his followers: Accept the daily privilege of God's fellowship without arrogance or selfishness. Over against the pride in a prominent place in the church or a fat offering, Micah urged: *"walk humbly with thy God."* Jimmy Carter realizes how difficult that is, how easily the pious can become proud of their humility! Once when evaluating his own involvement in Christian witnessing, he realized that he had met 300,000 people in behalf of his race for governor but had talked with only 140 for God in fourteen years.

In his book *Why Not the Best?* Carter tells of his experience as a visitor for his denomination in a Cuban and Puerto Rican neighborhood. His Navy Spanish was assisted by a Baptist partner named Eloy Cruz. At the end of their days together, Carter asked him "how a tough and rugged man like him could be so sensitive, kind, and filled with love. He was embarrassed by my question, but finally fumbled out an answer." In Spanish he said quietly: "Señor James, our Savior has hands which are very gentle, and he cannot do much with a man who is hard."[2]

Living by this three-part pattern from Micah shows greater devotion to God than elaborate rituals and costly religious facilities. "He hath showed thee, O man, what is good."

---

1. Tom Collins, *The Search for Jimmy Carter* (Waco, Texas: Word Books, 1976), p. 122.
2. Nashville, Tenn.: Broadman Press, 1975, p. 131.